A
BETTER
COUNTRY

Also by Dan Schaeffer

Defining Moments: When Choices Matter Most

In Search of . . . the Real Spirit of Christmas

When Faith and Decisions Collide: Finding God's Will for Your Life

A
BETTER
COUNTRY

Preparing for
Heaven

DAN
SCHAEFFER

DISCOVERY HOUSE
PUBLISHERS

Discovery House Publishers is affiliated with RBC Ministries,
Grand Rapids, Michigan.

Discovery House books are distributed to the trade exclusively by
Barbour Publishing, Inc., Uhrichsville, Ohio.

Requests for permission to quote from this book should be directed to: Permissions Department, Discovery House Publishers, P.O. Box 3566, Grand Rapids, MI 49501.

All Scripture quotations, unless otherwise indicated, are taken from the *Holy Bible, New International Version®. NIV®.* Copyright © 1973, 1978, 1984 by International Bible Society. Used by permission of Zondervan. All rights reserved.

Interior design by Sherri L. Hoffman

Library of Congress Cataloging-in-Publication Data
Schaeffer, Daniel, 1958-
 A better country : preparing for heaven / Dan Schaeffer.
 p. cm.
 ISBN: 978-1-57293-243-2
 1. Heaven—Christianity. 2. Future life—Christianity. I. Title
 BT846.3.S43 2008
 236'.24—dc22

PRINTED IN THE UNITED STATES OF AMERICA

09 10 11 12 / BPI / 10 9 8 7 6 5 4 3

TABLE OF CONTENTS

DEDICATION

This book is dedicated to the saints at Shoreline Community Church in Santa Barbara, California. It was during my ministry here that whispers of that better country began to beckon me. Your warm response and enthusiasm for the series on the better country encouraged me on this project. As we each draw nearer to that wonderful place, let our hearts become tuned more and more to that which lies ahead, not that which lies behind. The journey continues.

PART ONE
Heavenly Desire

The thing we've always wanted

CHAPTER ONE

A Better Country

They were longing for *a better country*—a heavenly one . . .
(HEBREWS 11:16).

These words from the book of Hebrews have teased and excited me for years, and I've found myself revisiting them time and again. They whisper to my soul, promising to whisk me away to a place I've never been, a place where I will finally be at peace, a place where everything will be perfect—a place of rest, joy, and unending adventure. They speak to a restless yearning in my soul, and I draw comfort that others have felt the same thing. Perhaps you've felt it. If not, I pray that you soon will. You will find yourself in good company.

Others before us—Noah, Abraham, Isaac, Jacob, Moses, Rahab, David, Samuel, the prophets, and many more—found themselves seeking, thinking, and desiring this better country, a world vastly different from the one they were experiencing. Their excitement about their lives extended well beyond their earthly existence; they longed to peek behind the veil that separates this life from the next. That other world—vibrant, alive, beautiful, unending, perfect, and, yes, mysterious—became the focus of their life, an attraction rather than a distraction.

Even while he lived in the Promised Land, Abraham was looking forward to living in another country. But it was no ordinary country: "for he was looking for the city which has foundations, whose architect and builder is God" (Hebrews 11:10 NASB).

All the men and women of faith were. No matter how good or bad things seemed in their particular situation, they realized that as long as they were alive on earth, they weren't really home. They were exiles and strangers in a foreign land and content with that, knowing that God had a special place waiting for them. They weren't far from home.

For years we have been warned, "Be careful of being so heavenly minded that you are no earthly good." Most of the Christians I've met are in little danger of that. They think such small, impoverished thoughts about heaven, yet most will profess that they can't wait to get there. You will often find, however, that someone's desire to go to heaven is far more attached to some current trial or suffering they want to escape on earth rather than a desire for their idea of heaven itself. When the trial passes and their earthly lives get better, often their passionate desire to go to heaven subsides. Heaven, for some, is mere escapism from trouble.

But, for the record, it is absolutely impossible to be so heavenly minded that you're no earthly good. That is, in fact, the very *opposite* of what the Bible teaches. We aren't told to put heaven out of our minds, or even aside for the moment, but in the very forefront of our thinking.

"Since, then, you have been raised with Christ, set your hearts on things above, where Christ is seated at the right hand of God. Set your minds on things above, not on earthly things" (Colossians 3:1–2).

Our outlook on the most important things in life springs from our understanding (or misunderstanding) of heaven. We can deal with the loss of our loved ones in Christ precisely because we believe we will see them again in heaven. We can deal with suffering and difficulty precisely because we take comfort that our present trouble in this life is temporary, but heaven and glory are forever; we can accept loss and reversal of fortunes precisely because our belief in heaven reminds us that our real treasure is in heaven where neither moth nor rust destroys (Matthew 6:19–20; Hebrews 10:32–39).

What caused the sadness in the rich young ruler when Jesus encouraged him to sell all he had, give it to the poor, and come and follow Him (Matthew 19:16–25)? It was his loose grip on the truth of heaven. This life was more real and immediate, and he could not, by faith, appropriate the reality and truth of heavenly certainties. Eventually, he would lose his earthly fortune upon his death, but unless he had a change of heart, he lost a heavenly one as a result. Among the several things that afflicted this man's thinking, a weak view of heaven was near the top.

It is a mistake to believe that our thoughts of heaven are irrelevant to our present lives. It is precisely your belief or doubt about the reality of heaven that drives many of your most important decisions and values.

Thinking about Heaven Is Not Escapism

"It's fascinating that the most important, most strategic, most enduring place in the universe gets so little attention," writes Joseph Stowell. "The moon and Mars get more press than heaven. Yet heaven is of unrivaled significance. When we stretch our view of life to embrace its reality, all of life is wonderfully rearranged."[1]

I have a friend who, when he was in his twenties, almost died. It made him completely re-assess his priorities and values. His appreciation of the tentative nature of his earthly life has brought the next life into much clearer focus. Ambition, such a temptation to men, no longer has the hold over him it could have. This life, he has learned, is temporary; eternity is forever. It has made him wise beyond his years.

An understanding of heaven is not a spiritual luxury; it is a spiritual necessity. It gives us the wisdom and insight to look at earthly success and failure as transient things. Heaven also gives us the necessary comfort that no matter how bad (or good) our present life is, there is a much better one coming.

"A continual looking forward to the eternal world is not a form of escapism or wishful thinking, but one of the things a Christian is meant to do," wrote scholar and philosopher C. S. Lewis. "It does not mean that we are to leave the present world as it is. If you read history, you will find that the Christians who did the most for the present world were just those who thought most of the next." [2]

Christian philosopher Peter Kreeft adds, "The . . . first question is not whether it is escapist but whether it is true. We cannot find out whether it is true simply by finding out whether it is escapist. "There is a tunnel under this prison" may be an escapist idea, but it may also be true."[3]

There are times here on earth when life is simply wonderful, and we can't imagine leaving it. There are other times when life is so painful it is difficult to bear another day. But even in the best of times, relationships are difficult, circumstances are unpredictable, health is a perpetual struggle, happiness takes wings, and deep down we long for a perfect life without stress and pain. What we're wishing for is what we were made for—the better country, even if we don't recognize it as that. I know for years I didn't recognize my longings as a desire for heaven.

Wrong Thoughts about Heaven Can Dilute Our Enthusiasm for It

Honestly, I wasn't always excited about the subject of heaven. This may sound like a strange confession for a pastor to make, but for many years I didn't seek, think about, or even desire heaven very much. For a long while I think it was because I didn't know quite what to think about it. My main instruction about heaven was that it existed, that it was surely a great place, and that little more could be known about it this side of life—so why bother speculating?

As a young boy, when I would hear things like "Heaven is a wonderful place" and "Everyone wants to go to heaven" from my Sunday school teachers, I'm embarrassed to say I wasn't among the "everyone" wanting to go to that wonderful place. Don't misunderstand, I believed in Jesus and certainly didn't want to go to hell, but, like many, I figured heaven was probably like Sunday school—which wasn't a ringing endorsement.

I didn't hate Sunday school, but it hardly compared with my excitement for other places and activities. As a young boy I used to run through the gently rolling, tree-covered hills of Santa Rosa, California, pretending to be an explorer or a cowboy or a great hunter. Living out in the country, I would discover places that I was sure no one had ever been before. I would startle herds of deer and spend hours climbing trees, catching lizards and field mice, and wondering what was over the next hill. Since I would much rather do that than go to Sunday school, I wasn't too keen on heaven, or at least on arriving any earlier than necessary.

Then, years later, when as a pastor I began to speak to people about heaven, I found I had little to add to my Sunday school instruction. Strangely, in the Bible institute and seminary I attended, we didn't talk much about heaven. We talked an awful lot about how one gets there, but very little about what "there" was like. Only now, in retrospect, does that seem strange. While I desperately wanted to be rid of my sin nature and be with Christ, I had little other itinerary for heaven. What would I find in heaven that would excite me—*forever*? That's both a tall order and an intimidating prospect. Forever is a very, very long time to live anywhere. What if I got bored after the first million years? Though it may sound slightly sacrilegious to say that, it's a serious consideration.

Earth is familiar. Earth is home. Earth we love.

Then, quite accidentally, I stumbled upon some passages in Revelation that provided a glimpse into heaven that both surprised and delighted me. My interest in heaven was suddenly piqued because I began to realize it was not what I had expected. I began to wonder how much about heaven I could learn from the biblical evidence we have. As I studied and began to realize more of what heaven was going to be like and what God's purpose for me here and forever was, I began slowly shifting my priorities. I no longer live for this life alone.

I think if the truth were known, many Christians are at best ambivalent about, or at worst afraid of, heaven—or at least of the vision of it they have in their minds. There used to be an old game show where you had to pick the prize behind door number one, door number two, or door number three. Behind only one of those doors was there something valuable. Behind two of them was something worthless. Many people, sadly even many Christians, are afraid of what might be behind the door they open into eternity. We're far more attached to earth than we think. This may partly explain why it can be so hard to get Christians to think beyond this earthly life to greater spiritual realities and to sacrifice too many of this world's goods for the sake of the eternal kingdom.

Wrong Thoughts of Heaven Can Make Us Homesick for Earth

The idea that heaven is some*where* and some*thing* other than earthly tends to make us nostalgic for earth even as we talk about heaven. While a part of us is certainly excited about the idea of being with Jesus, having our sin nature removed, and living with Him forever, if we're honest, a part of us is also already homesick for earth—and we feel guilty even thinking that. The idea that one day we won't see a sunset over the ocean or gaze on a forest of ancient redwoods or see the leaves turn colors during a New England fall or cuddle a puppy or sit by a cozy fireplace on a rainy night with loved ones seems terribly sad.

Thoughts of heaven might even prompt regret about what we'll never be able to do. I myself have realized that I might never one day get to Ireland or Scotland or Switzerland or England as I had hoped. I might never gaze across the vast Canadian tundra or watch grizzly bears catching salmon along an Alaskan river. I've gazed at the Milky Way and seen the desert sky filled with stars, but I've always wanted to see the Aurora Borealis. It might not happen. I've raised three children, but I might not get to see my grandchildren or their children. I'll miss fly-fishing on the Merced River in Yosemite and riding my bike with my wife in our beautiful Santa Ynez Valley wine country. I'll miss oak trees and deer grazing in the meadows and hawks soaring overhead and the brilliant sunset as night falls.

We comfort ourselves with the thought that in heaven we'll feel no loss or regrets, but it doesn't remove the sad nostalgia we feel now. Our desire for heaven is not based on our revulsion for earth but for the curse of sin that has afflicted our life on earth. If the truth were told, we'd be perfectly happy if God decided to stick with earth and just get rid of the curse of sin that makes living here so painful and dangerous. Most of us would vote to have Eden restored on earth rather than spend eternity in some unknown celestial city in the sky. If you've ever felt that way, I've got some good news for you—that is *precisely* what God has been planning to do all along.

Wrong Thoughts about Heaven Have Gotten Good Press

Heaven has been characterized in movie after movie and book after book as an eternal existence in a sterile, white, mostly cloudy place with emotionless angels playing harp music (probably classical). And, frankly, many of us, if we were honest, can only sigh and think, "Well, at least it isn't hell." Others aren't so sure.

Only recently authorities in Australia have been blaring music by singers Barry Manilow and Doris Day into a suburban Sydney park frequented by late-night revelers in an attempt to discourage them from coming and being a nuisance to the local citizenry. It is proving to be effective in driving the revelers off, but now citizens of the suburb are complaining about the music—and it's scheduled to go on for six more months! To many, this would seem like an appropriate preview for heaven, as they know it. Music they can't stand going on forever!

Mark Twain, the brilliant humorist, described his vision of heaven and its heavenly music. "It goes on all day long, and every day, during a stretch of twelve hours. The singing of hymns alone, nay, it is of one hymn alone. The words are always the same; in number they are only about a dozen; there is no rhyme, there is no poetry."[4] One of Twain's beloved main characters, Huck Finn, shares the instruction he received about heaven from his guardian, Miss Watson: "Now she had got a start, and she went on and told me all about the good place. She said all a body would have to do there was to go around all day long with a harp and sing, forever and ever. So I didn't think much of it."[5]

Perhaps not too strangely, hell has been made to look more attractive than heaven to many people. (When Huck Finn asked Miss Watson if Tom Sawyer was going to heaven, she told him no, which made Huck glad—he wanted to go where Tom went.) The stereotype of pure Hugh Hefner hedonism, erotica, and party-on-forever atmosphere sounds better than heaven to some people. It may be where the bad people go, but the truth is that it can seem a lot more exciting than many of our distorted views of heaven. With a little air conditioning, it might be preferable.

But *is* heaven an ethereal place where disembodied spirits of religious zealots, Eagle Scouts, philanthropists, and church do-gooders go to live out their reward on clouds in the sky while harp music plays in the background—*forever*?

Hardly. And it's about time we started thinking far more seriously about heaven as Christians. Even secular writers are tiring of the watered-down versions of heaven we are offered. Op-ed columnist for the *New York Times*, David Brooks, wrote a March 9, 2004, article entitled, "Hooked on Heaven Lite," partly in response to Mitch Albom's book, *The Five People You Meet in Heaven.* In his article Brooks complains from a secular perspective about the views of heaven that are promoted to the public. Albom's book's main character is an 83-year-old man who feels lonely, adrift, and unimportant and dies trying to save a little girl from a broken carnival ride. Brooks begins talking about the main character.

> He goes to heaven and meets five people who tell him that he is
> not alone and that his life was not unimportant. They reconcile him
> with his father, who had been cruel to him. They remind him of what

a good person he was. He gets to spend time with his wife, whom he'd neglected and who died young. He is forgiven for the hurts he accidentally committed while alive.

Responding to this view of heaven, Brooks writes,

All societies construct their own images of heaven. Most imagine a wondrous city or a verdant garden where human beings come face to face with God. But the heaven that is apparently popular with readers these days is nothing more than an excellent therapy session. In Albom's book, God, to the extent that he exists there, is sort of a genial Dr. Phil. When you go to his heaven, friends and helpers come and tell you how innately wonderful you are. They help you reach closure. In this heaven, God and his glory are not the center of attention. It's all about you.

Here, sins are not washed away. Instead, hurt is washed away. The language of good and evil is replaced by the language of trauma and recovery. There is no vice and virtue, no moral framework to locate the individual within the cosmic infinity of the universe. Instead there are just the right emotions — Do you feel good about yourself? — buttressed by an endless string of vague bromides about how special each person is, and how much we are all mystically connected in the flowing river of life.

"Plagued by anxiety, depression, vague discontents, a sense of inner emptiness, the 'psychological man' of the 20th century seeks neither individual self-aggrandizement nor spiritual transcendence but peace of mind, under conditions that increasingly militate against it," Christopher Lasch wrote in "The Culture of Narcissism." Lasch went on to call the therapeutic mentality an anti-religion that tries to liberate people from the idea that they should submit to a higher authority, so they can focus more obsessively on their own emotional needs.

Reading *The Five People You Meet in Heaven* is a sad experience because it conjures up a mass of people who, like its hero, feel lonely and unimportant. But instead of offering them the rich moral framework of organized religion or rigorous philosophy, instead of reminding them of the tough-minded exemplars of the Bible and history, books like Albom's throw the seekers remorselessly back upon themselves . . .

Americans in the 21st century are more likely to be divorced from any sense of a creedal order, ignorant of the moral traditions that have come down to us through the ages and detached from the sense that we all owe obligations to a higher authority.

Wrong thoughts about heaven have gotten good press, but they haven't made heaven look any more attractive. Is it any wonder few are interested in the subject? It is definitely time we started thinking far more about heaven than we have in the past.

Thinking Seriously about Heaven

If we decide to go on vacation for several weeks, we will often spend many days, even weeks, studying our chosen destination. What will it be like? How should we dress? What should we bring? What's there to see? We study brochures, pictures, and travel guides and search the Internet to gather all the information we can. After all, we'll be there two weeks! But how much do average Christians know about where they'll spend *forever*?

If you ask the average Christian what heaven is going to be like, you often get little more than "It's going to be beautiful," or "It will be perfect." Certainly we know that emotionally we'll be far better off, but there tends to be very little discussion of anything more specific since we've become hesitant to consider clear biblical allusions to heaven as anything more than symbolic. But what will it be like to live there? The fear of boredom haunts many of our thoughts of heaven. Temporary earthly suffering—no matter how bad—is actually preferable to eternal boredom, for the suffering, as bad as it may be, will at some point cease. But if we become bored in heaven, *eternally*, what is there to save us?

How many of us would sign up to visit a resort or vacation destination whose only advertising was "It's beautiful, just perfect," but provides us with no details? You have no idea what the resort looks like or what it offers. The ads may say it's perfect—but perfect for whom? It may indeed be perfect—for hikers—but what if you're not a hiker? Or it may be perfect for hunters or surfers, but what if you're neither? What if it's designed for senior citizens and you're twenty-something, or for kids and you're eighty?

To be properly excited about going somewhere, we need to know something about where we're going. We love pictures, descriptions, testimonies from folks who've been there, and an idea of what there is to do once we've arrived. Without this information our excitement dims considerably, especially when the place we're thinking about lasts forever. In fact, just saying that word can make us nervous. Forever! That's a *very* long time. In fact, it's a fixed point at which the passing of time ceases to be meaningful. Fortunately, Scripture provides us with quite a bit of information about heaven.

Which Heaven?

This is a good time to stop and explain that the Bible uses the term *heaven* in three separate and distinct ways.

1. The *atmospheric* heaven. The word *heaven* can be used to refer to the sky, the space surrounding the earth to a height of six miles (Deuteronomy 33:13; Isaiah 55:10). This is the idea of looking into the "heavenlies."
2. The *celestial* heaven. This refers to the realm of sun, moon, stars, planets, and galaxies (Genesis 1:1; Psalm 33:6).
3. The dwelling place of God. This is what Paul was referring to in 2 Corinthians 12:2 as the "third heaven" and what Jesus called paradise (Psalm 2:4; Isaiah 66:1; Matthew 6:9; Revelation 4:1ff.).

It is in this third sense that we are speaking of heaven as our better country, the dwelling place of God, the place Jesus has gone to prepare for us to live with Him (John 14:1–4).

Your greatest ambitions and adventures on earth will pale next to what lies ahead in the better country. Your deepest joy and greatest longings on earth will lose their luster when you discover what God has planned—and this is only from the teasers God has provided for us in the Scriptures.

The reality will be infinitely better than our finite minds could possibly comprehend on this side. Maybe more importantly, when you begin to learn what God has planned for you, your understanding of His infinite, tender, eternal, and unconditional love for you will become much clearer.

You will realize how much God loves you and how He's planned to continue doing that—forever.

Heaven will be perfect for you, because the One who made both you and it is perfect. Joys you haven't even imagined, ambition you never thought in your wildest dreams you could fulfill, and unending discovery of your new eternal world and its eternal creator are your future. The creator of heaven Himself will show you the wonders of it. God made us for earth, and He knew we'd love it. He was right. The better country was made for you as well, but it is, by definition, *better by far*! Just let that sink in. In C. S. Lewis's classic fiction book, *The Last Battle*, Lewis describes the difference between old Narnia and new Narnia (heaven).

> The difference between the old Narnia and the New Narnia was like that. The newer one was a deeper country: every rock and flower and blade of grass looked as if it meant more. I can't describe it any better than that: if you ever get there, you will know what I mean. It was the Unicorn who summed up what everyone was feeling. He stamped his right fore-hoof on the ground and neighed and then cried: "I have come home at last. This is my real country! I belong here. This is the land I have been looking for all my life, though I never knew it till now. The reason why we loved the old Narnia is that it sometimes looked a little like this. Bree-hee-hee—Come further up, come further in."[6]

The beautiful country that the "great cloud of witnesses" looked forward to is real, tangible, and exciting. The Bible tells us far more about the better country than many of us realize. If you are a Christian, it is *your* country; you're already a citizen. It will be, in a strange way, both new and familiar. Your personal and unique home is there, yours alone, designed for you by the God who loved you enough to die for you and who rose again from the dead as a promise and proof of the resurrection to come. If you aren't yet a Christian, this book will be a trailer of coming attractions, giving you an opportunity to understand what the Bible means when it speaks about heaven.

Preparing today for heaven is one of our main callings as Christians. Some of us may be entering the better country soon; others will have a wait. For myself, I am growing impatient, especially after exploring what the Bible says about my real country. We certainly won't be able to see or understand everything, but even glimpses of it will change your life.

I'm preparing for heaven. I hope you'll join me as we go exploring our better country. What we will discover will change your life forever. So let's begin our journey of discovery together.

Let's go further up and further into . . . *the better country*.

CHAPTER TWO

Heaven on My Mind

If I find in myself a desire which no experience in this world can satisfy, the most probable explanation is that I was made for another world.[1]   — C. S. LEWIS

If you ask most people if they think much about heaven, they will most likely tell you no and mean it. Even Christians, who are counting on spending eternity in heaven, won't answer all that differently, if they're honest. But the problem is not that they aren't thinking about heaven very much but that they don't know it when they are.

We are often asking the question the wrong way. We have forgotten that we are made in the image of God and that He is an eternal being. Within us there is restlessness with the life we are now living because, frankly, it's not the one we were originally designed for. Even in our sinful shortened life, we bear the memory imprint of the life and place God designed us for. A duck can be born and raised and never see a pond or lake for years. But if ever it sees a small puddle, it is attracted to it without knowing why. Every instinct in its body is attracted to water, even if it doesn't understand it. It's the same with us.

If you want to know if people ever think about heaven, just ask them if they ever feel like life should be a lot different from what it is. Ask them if they get frustrated because of problems and wish life didn't have to be like this. Ask them if they could change their world in a number of significant ways, how they would do it. Very soon you will have them talking about heaven—*the way they think life should be.* Their ideas may not be that well thought out, but they will be heartfelt. And they will not simply reflect their selfish desires, but also their inherited creative design. They can imagine a life far different from the one they are currently experiencing. Though we often aren't aware of it, we have heaven on our minds far more frequently than we imagine.

As a pastor, I have performed many funerals over the years. It is in these tragic moments in peoples' lives that they most clearly articulate their ideas of heaven. And I learn again and again that the desire for heaven is intense and universal, but our understanding of heaven is weak and muddled.

Ideas of Heaven

Reporter and journalist Barbara Walters interviewed a number of people several years ago, trying to answer this question: What is heaven like, and who gets to go there? While she doesn't believe in heaven herself, she admitted that there was a great deal of interest in spirituality. Why are we here? Where are we going? She acknowledged even before she began her study that most of us, regardless of our religious persuasion, do not think that life ends here. We simply do not believe that this life is all there is.

Her project took her an entire year, and writer Gail Cameron Wescott summarized Walters's findings in a *Reader's Digest* article (December 2005). Walters began by interviewing a seventeen-year-old Palestinian terrorist in a maximum-security Israeli prison who had attempted to detonate a bomb on a crowded street. He believes his reward will be to enter paradise, where he will enjoy joyous sex on silken couches amid rivers of milk and honey. Muslims believe that paradise is a place of lavishly comfortable homes with beautiful gardens and servants to attend them. Food and wine will be plentiful, and both men and women will equally enjoy sex in a hedonistic pleasure. As strange as it may seem, what drove this young man to attempt to commit this heinous act was his idea of heaven and his longing to go there. Heaven can be a far more powerful motivator than we imagine, both for good and for evil.

There are over ten thousand religions in the world, and almost all believe in some sort of afterlife. Furthermore, statistics tell us that nine out of ten people surveyed believe that heaven is a real place—and that they are going there!

But where is *there*? *What* is there?

Anthony DeStefano, author of A *Travel Guide to Heaven*, believes that in the afterlife we'll be able to go fishing with Ernest Hemingway and study piano with Mozart and painting with Michelangelo, provided, of course, that these folks actually made it to heaven themselves.

To many people, heaven is just an amalgam of all our favorite unattainable earthly desires. Whatever you really like on earth will be waiting for you in heaven. At funerals of cowboys or surfers, for example, we might hear of the deceased now riding the heavenly range or surfing the ultimate wave in heaven.

But is heaven simply the fulfillment of our earthly fantasies? If we always wanted to play the piano, will we get to learn from Mozart? If we admired Ernest Hemingway, will we be able to take fishing lessons from him in heaven? Forget for the moment the issue of whether either Mozart or Hemingway will be in heaven at all—what if Mozart doesn't want to give piano lessons to millions of people forever? Would that be Mozart's idea of heaven? What if Hemingway's vision of heaven is to go fishing alone? With this approach, heaven is, in actuality, nothing. Unless you believe that there are billions of virgins with no greater desire for all eternity than to fulfill some Muslim man's (or woman's, for that matter) desire for sex, unless you believe that heaven is at the same time a huge ranch in the sky and nothing but miles of coastline producing perfect waves, we have a problem.

If Heaven Is Everything, It Is Nothing

Using this approach, then, heaven is either everything everyone ever wanted (which creates problems because our desires often conflict with one another's), or it's nothing more than fertile and reaching imagination. Besides, whatever personal vision we might have of heaven will necessarily involve an actual place that has been created for us. Who has the power to create such a place? It doesn't make a lot of sense just to say it will appear because we really want it to. We are definitely speaking of another worldly place, which necessitates other worldly beings and a creator.

The assumption behind all this thinking is that whoever made this heaven has no greater priority than seeking to ensure that all our earthly fantasies are fulfilled forever. Most people would get quiet if you asked them why they believe they deserve such a reward. It just seems to be an assumption that if I can dream of it and want it badly enough, somehow I deserve it.

There seems to be a very strong dose of American and Western consumerism in many modern versions of heaven. Soon, heaven becomes merely a catalog of the best earthly delights we can imagine, where all we need to do is make our choice before departure, place our order, and then attempt to be reasonably well behaved until it's time for our reward.

The idea is that if we get the thing we always wanted on earth in heaven, we'll be happy forever. Here's the problem.

It isn't true.

It doesn't work.

It's a pipe dream.

Take your choice.

Getting Everything You Want Isn't Enough

Many of us have never realized our greatest dreams and fantasies. We weren't the most beautiful or the most talented, the best athlete, musician, performer, or student. But *someone* was! There are a few, a precious few, who actually did get it all. All they could dream of receiving—the money, the fame, the trophy spouse, the lifestyle, the body, the brain, the whole package. You could almost say they were able to experience this idea of heaven—where you get all your fantasies met—on earth. The problem is that over and over you hear the same thing: It isn't enough.

Actor Jim Carrey said recently, "I think everybody should get rich and famous and do everything they ever dreamed of so they can see that it's not the answer."[2] History shows us that many of those who have what we think we'd need to be truly happy forever are the most miserable.

In an interview on 60 *Minutes*, Tom Brady, the New England Patriots star quarterback, winner of three Super Bowls before turning thirty, tried to explain what was bothering him. "Why do I have three Super Bowl rings and still think there is something greater out there for me? A lot of people would say, 'This is what it is. I reached my goal, my dream. It's got to be more than this. I mean, this isn't what it's all cracked up to be.'"[3]

Pop star Ricky Martin says the fame and fortune he experienced in the late nineties left him feeling bored and embittered. "There was a moment when I was onstage and I was just so angry," he says in *People* magazine. "I thought, 'Something is wrong. I have the applause, I have a great band behind me, I live comfortably . . . I was starting to become a victim of fame . . . I wasn't enjoying it."[4]

Actress Winona Ryder, who starred in *Beetlejuice, Mermaids,* Bram Stoker's *Dracula,* and *Little Women* thought she had it all. She was famous, making lots of money, and was romantically involved with actor Johnny Depp. But it wasn't enough. She shared in an interview in October 2000, "When I was 18, I was driving around at two in the morning, completely crying and alone and scared. I drove by this magazine stand that has this *Rolling Stone* that I was on the cover of, and it said, 'Winona Ryder: The Luckiest Girl in the World.' And there I was feeling more alone than I ever had."[5]

Scott Donie, a diver, emerged from nowhere in the 1992 Olympics in Barcelona, Spain. No one expected Donie to perform well, but he came home with a silver medal. Donie later said, "That was a perfect day for me, everything clicked." But later, instead of feeling great, he began to feel terrible. The fame and fortune he had expected eluded him. Worse, every time he climbed onto the deck, he was expected to perform as well as he had in the Olympics. The pressure almost caused him to leave the sport altogether. He later said, "It's ironic that all your life you know what you want to be and then you become it and you get all sad and depressed . . . You don't know why you're feeling that way. It's a feeling that comes from nowhere. It seems like a chemical."[6] There are more cases like this, and new ones occur every day.

"What does not satisfy when we find it, was not the thing we were desiring."[7]

We have too many earthly examples showing us that this idea of heaven won't fit the bill of "happily ever after." In short, earthly desires, even when fulfilled, leave us longing for more—for something else, something transcendent. An eternal existence of unfulfilled desire, where you have all you could possibly want of earthly pleasures and find yourself growing more and more dissatisfied, is less a description of heaven than a description of hell. It is the stuff of Rod Serling, not the God of the Bible.

I happen to love chocolate—almost any type. But I've noticed that when I have chocolate in abundance, I start to get sick of it. And that's on earth where my lifespan is, if I'm blessed, eighty years or so. Those who indulge in free and unrestrained sexual activity or substance abuse or the adrenaline chase inevitably experience the same thing. Chocolate, sex, adventure, and accomplishment produce pleasure—but only for a while. When we exercise self-control and holy restraint in these pleasures, they continue to please us, but that means that part of our pleasure is not in the actual experience, but in the anticipation of it. It means far more to us when we deny ourselves the constant experience.

Homesick for Eden

"No one can live without delight," writes Peter Kreeft, "and that is why a man, deprived of spiritual joy goes over to carnal pleasures."[8]

So much of our life, both joys and temptations, are related to our longing to return to Eden. Our present sinful human nature is unable to truly satisfy itself with earthly pleasures alone. Therefore a heaven where our greatest earthly fantasies and desires are our external reward seems like a sure recipe for discontentment—*forever*. Put simply, it would be a bad idea that omniscience would recognize right away.

While all of these, and thousands of other, ideas of heaven are not at all what the Bible teaches, they do point to the fact that every person is made in the image of God, so this desire for eternality, immortality, perfection, lasting peace, and eternal joy is hardwired into every person's spiritual DNA.

"Most of us find it very difficult to want 'Heaven' at all," wrote C. S. Lewis, "except in so far as 'Heaven' means meeting again our friends who have died. One reason for this difficulty is that we have not been trained: our whole education tends to fix our minds on this world. Another reason is that when the real want for Heaven is present in us, we do not recognize it. Most people, if they had really learned to look into their own hearts, would know that they do want, and want acutely, something that cannot be had in this world. There are all sorts of things in this world that offer to give it to you, but they never quite keep their promise."[9]

Solomon, in Ecclesiastes, reminds us that God "has also set eternity in the hearts of men" (Ecclesiastes 3:11).

We long for heaven simply because we were made for it. We, who were originally designed by God for Eden, an eternal existence in a perfect place, still feel the pull inside of us for the life we were designed for. Though we lost that perfect existence, we can still feel the loss. We want to return to Eden. Whether we know it or not, eternity is whispering to us continually, even if we don't completely understand it. What God has placed inside of us cannot be turned off; it can only be tuned out.

"So it is that men sigh on, not knowing what the soul wants, but only that it needs something," wrote Henry Ward Beecher. "Our yearnings are homesickness for heaven. Our sighings are sighings for God just as children that cry themselves to sleep away from home and sob in their slumber, not knowing that they sob for their parents. The soul's inarticulate moanings are the affections, yearning for the Infinite, and having no one to tell them what ails them." [10]

This desire to have a life that is perfect forever is normal. It is normal because you were designed for it. Put in another way, the frustration we feel when things go badly, when we get sick, when pain and suffering come upon us is but a different form of the same desire for the life we were designed for. We get frustrated because we feel that life really shouldn't be like this. And we're right. What we have is a holy discontentment.

A Holy Discontentment

We are trying to capture something elusive. "Nobody ever gets through the tiny gate into the secret garden. Nobody ever hears the horns of elfland, or finds the faerie sea. The closest we ever get to it all is some hint or echo in a face or a painting or a concerto or a woodland glade, and then it fills us with an infinite sadness, because we know that it is lost, and that we must turn back to our traffic jams and enemas and red tape." [11]

That is why when we get older and can no longer do what we used to, we lament the loss of physical youth. We lament it because we can still feel so young inside. Our spirit, which was made in God's image, is immortal. It cannot age; it was made eternal, which is why when our bodies are weary of life, our spirits can long so desperately to live.

There is a part of us, an important part, that longs for and dreams of life on earth *as it could be*. This desire for what we can't have on earth here has led many Christians to feel a bit guilty when they are feeling less than fulfilled with their current status. We are often led to believe that we should be totally fulfilled here on earth, and if we're not, something's wrong with us. We must not be spiritual enough.

If we are constantly seeking to have more comforts and luxuries and grow envious of those who have more than we do, our lack of contentment is curable. We need a change of heart and mind—and mostly a change of perspective. On the other hand, there is a lingering discontentment (that will ebb and flow over our lifespan) with living in a fallen sinful world that is not only to be expected but is completely understandable and valid. Many Scriptures echo and affirm that these feelings aren't wrong; they are simply the righteous longing for the better country we were designed for. You aren't the only one who has felt them; in fact, you are in very good company, as you will see.

"For to me, to live is Christ and to die is gain. If I am to go on living in the body, this will mean fruitful labor for me. *Yet what shall I choose? I do not know! I am torn between the two: I desire to depart and be with Christ, which is better by far*; but it is more necessary for you that I remain in the body" (Philippians 1:21–24, emphasis added). The great apostle Paul, who had seen heaven up close and personal (2 Corinthians 12:1–5), wanted to go back! His desire was to depart and be with Christ, which he knew by experience was "better by far." He was, like those before him, thinking of the better country. It was now imprinted on his heart and mind.

Why does the author of Hebrews remind us that the saints of old admitted that they were "aliens and strangers on earth" (11:13)? Moses himself never entered the Promised Land; he was permitted to see it only from the mountaintops of Moab (Numbers 27:12; Deuteronomy 3:27). Throughout his life, Moses was nothing more than a stranger, a wanderer who moved from Egypt to Midian and eventually the border of Canaan. To the day of his death he remained an alien and stranger. His faith persevered because "he saw him who is invisible" (Hebrews 11:27).

But Moses wasn't alone.

"*I am an alien and stranger among you*," Abraham confessed to the Hittites (Genesis 23:4, emphasis added).

"So Jacob said to Pharaoh, '*The years of my sojourning* are one hundred and thirty' " (Genesis 47:9, emphasis added).

Speaking to the Lord, David confesses, "We are aliens and strangers in your sight, *as were all our forefathers*. Our days on earth are like a shadow" (1 Chronicles 29:15, emphasis added).

Again, in Psalms, David confesses to the Lord: "Hear my prayer, O Lord, listen to my cry for help; be not deaf to my weeping. *For I dwell with you as an alien, a stranger, as all my fathers were*" (Psalm 39:12, italics added).

It was Peter who proclaimed to the church, "Dear friends, *I urge you, as aliens and strangers in the world*, to abstain from sinful desires, which war against your soul" (1 Peter 2:11, emphasis added). He urges us to action based upon our identity as aliens and strangers in this world.

Paul writes to the Corinthian church:

> Now we know that if the earthly tent we live in is destroyed, we have a building from God, an eternal house in heaven, not built by human hands. *Meanwhile we groan, longing to be clothed with our heavenly dwelling*, because when we are clothed, we will not be found naked. For while we are in this tent, *we groan and are burdened, because we do not wish to be unclothed but to be clothed with our heavenly dwelling, so that what is mortal may be swallowed up by life. Now it is God who has made us for this very purpose* and has given us the Spirit as a deposit, guaranteeing what is to come. Therefore we are always confident and know that as long as we are at home in the body we are away from the Lord. We live by faith, not by sight. *We are confident I say, and would prefer to be away from the body and at home with the Lord*" (2 Corinthians 5:1–9, italics added).

To the Romans Paul writes, "We ourselves, who have the firstfruits of the Spirit, *groan inwardly as we wait eagerly for our adoption as sons, the redemption of our bodies*. For in this hope we were saved. But hope that is seen is no hope at all. Who hopes for what he already has? But if we hope for what we do not yet have, we wait for it patiently" (Romans 8:23–25, italics added). Desire is articulated so clearly by Paul; our very beings groan for relief from the distress of the curse of sin in our world. We experience a holy discontentment because our soul's inner and deepest desires cannot find fulfillment in our present world.

We're Not Really at Home—Not Yet

"Alienation is the opposite of being at home," writes Peter Kreeft. "If the Bible is not wrong when it calls us strangers and pilgrims, then that's why we feel alienation: we feel what is. When any organism is at home, there is an ecological fit with its environment, a harmony, a rightness. If the environment does not supply this, that environment is not its home."[12]

This is why, at times, we feel so alienated from the world we live in, even while we love the earth and world itself. The place is familiar and dear to us, but we recognize that sin has ruined any chance of lasting happiness here.

A 1985 fantasy film called *Ladyhawke* tells the story of a strong and noble warrior and his beautiful lover, separated by a terrible curse. A jealous, crazed clergyman who wanted the woman's love himself sought the powers of darkness to create a curse that would separate the lovers forever. The curse caused the warrior to turn into a wolf by night and the woman to turn into a hawk by day. As night became day, in that moment between darkness and dawn, the two could catch a glimpse of the other in human form. They would gaze longingly at each other and reach out, but in the next moment, they would each be changed again. It caused them agony because what they longed for was so close and yet so unattainable.

That's the way we are on earth; while here, we get glimpses of heaven, tastes of eternity, moments when we feel exhilaration beyond words, but then it is gone much too quickly. It can be brought on by something in nature, something in our relationships with others, or just something in private reflection, but sadly, it doesn't linger long, and then it's gone.

Glimpses of Heaven

My wife and I recently went on vacation to Maui, a long overdue break from the grinding routine of life and work. We hadn't been on a real vacation in three years, and our batteries were dangerously low. The flurry of activity preceding our departure had been frantic, and we wanted nothing more than to just relax. Since we had been to Maui five years before, our only goal was to relax, not sightsee.

One evening we drove from our hotel a few miles to the quaint historical whaling harbor town of Lahaina. We walked slowly along the wooden

boardwalk fronting the many tourist shops of the small town, trying to decide where to get some dinner. We hadn't made reservations, so we knew
we'd have a wait. We had several restaurants to choose from. Annette
chose a restaurant on the ocean side of the street, hoping that we might
be able to at least see the ocean from our table.

At the restaurant we were informed that there was one table available that would allow one of us to have a good view of the ocean and the
other a good view of the other person. While waiting only a minute for
our table, the lovely young hostess informed us that a "good" table had
just opened up and beckoned us to follow her. Our "good" table was at
the balcony directly overlooking the ocean. The beautiful Hawaiian sky
was piercingly blue and peaceful, and we had an unobstructed view of the
island of Lanai across the channel. The tiki torches were lit, and as we
were escorted to our seats, the young hostess put her hand on each of our
shoulders and said quietly, "Eat slowly, and enjoy the sunset."

Several small sailboats bobbed lazily at anchor as the long gentle
waves rolled quietly in. The warm Hawaiian trade winds were blowing
softly as the sun slowly descended behind a small copse of palm trees. For
the first time in a long while, we were completely and totally relaxed. We
had nowhere to go and nothing to do. We could actually enjoy the moment—savor it, in fact. It was a strange experience.

Beneath us, on the first floor of the restaurant, a velvety voiced Hawaiian crooner began singing softly. Our dinner was delicious, and we
did indeed eat slowly, savoring every morsel and remembering again what
life was like without the pressure, the difficult decisions, and the stress of
everyday life. As the sun began to dip below the horizon in a beautiful
sunset, our Hawaiian crooner began to sing the song "What a Wonderful
World" by Louis Armstrong. The lyrics describe the beauty of green trees,
red roses, the sky, the clouds, rainbows, the fellowship of friends—all of
the things that truly make life on this earth wonderful. Each verse ends
with the line, "I think to myself, what a wonderful world."

I sighed inwardly, long and meaningfully. It was such a blessed moment. These precious, fleeting moments, which happen so infrequently,
become imprinted on our memories forever. They remind us that we do
indeed, at times, love this world very much. It is a reminder of the lost
promise of Eden.

Everyone was enjoying the moment around us. Pictures were being snapped, toasts made, laughter and cheerful talk filled the room, enhancing the mood. For that brief Camelot moment, all was right with our tiny slice of life. It was also a reminder of what we lost, what we could have had were it not for sin.

Lewis wrote, "Our Father refreshes us on the journey with some pleasant inns, but will not encourage us to mistake them for home."[13] Each of us has experienced some of these "pleasant inn" moments. They are some of our favorite memories, but what makes them so precious to us is that they are rare—too rare. They are tantalizing hors d'oeuvres to life in the better country, reminding us of the wonderful banquet to come. But they aren't the banquet. As good as they may seem at the moment, they don't last. But we want them to, don't we? A holy discontentment is natural in each one of us. In a strange way, restlessness is the right feeling for us.

"Rest along the way, premature rest, is danger; the way to true rest is restlessness."[14]

Were we never to read the Bible, the longing deep within us of a perfect world and a life without sorrow, pain, danger, death, trouble, and relational conflict would still burn bright. God has indeed set eternity in our hearts.

"The fact that we don't view death with optimism just might be because we think of death as taking us from our home, rather than bringing us to our home."[15]

The Argument from Desire

It was C. S. Lewis who articulated so clearly the argument for heaven from desire. In his book *Mere Christianity*, he posits that every natural or innate desire in us relates to a corresponding real object that can satisfy the desire. Since there exists in us a desire which nothing in time, nothing on earth, and no creature can satisfy, there must exist something outside of time, earth, and creatures that can satisfy this desire.

He suggests there are three different ways of looking at this:

1. The Fool's Way—He puts the blame on the things themselves. He goes on all his life thinking that if only he tried another woman, or went for a more expensive holiday, or whatever it is, then, this time, he really would catch the mysterious something we are all

after. Most of the bored, discontented, rich people in the world are of this type . . . always thinking that the latest is 'the Real Thing' at last, and always disappointed.

2. The Way of the Disillusioned "Sensible Man." He soon decides that the whole thing was moonshine. "Of course," he says, "one feels like that when one's young. But by the time you get to my age you've given up chasing the rainbow's end." And so he settles down and learns not to expect too much and represses the part of himself which used, as he would say, "to cry for the moon." . . . It would be the best line we could take if man did not live forever. But supposing infinite happiness really is there, waiting for us? Supposing one really can reach the rainbow's end? In that case it would be a pity to find out too late.

3. The Christian Way—The Christian says "Creatures are not born with desires unless satisfaction for those desires exists. A baby feels hunger: well, there is such a thing as food. A duckling wants to swim: well, there is such a thing as water. Men feel sexual desire: Well, there is such a thing as sex. If I find in myself a desire which no experience in this world can satisfy, the most probable explanation is that I was made for another world . . . I must keep alive in myself the desire for my true country, which I shall not find till after death; I must never let it get snowed under or turned aside; I must make it the main object of life to press on to that country and to help others to do the same."[16]

Whether you've known it or not, you've had heaven on your mind many times. Like most of us, you couldn't articulate it clearly. But once you recognize that voice, that whisper from the far-off country, you will hear it far more often. It will seem closer. And you won't mistake it for anything else. The desire is real, and nothing else in this life can satisfy it. That is both comforting and invigorating.

Heaven: It is the thing you've always wanted. But what about this better country—this world we've always longed for. Where is it? What is it like?

"God is at home; we are in the Far Country" (Saint John the Divine).

The journey continues.

PART TWO

Heavenly Location

The world we've always longed for

CHAPTER THREE

Heaven on Earth—*Finally*

But in keeping with his promise we are looking forward to
a new heaven and a new earth, the home of righteousness
(2 PETER 3:13).

W e often hear people talking about making a heaven on earth. We
realize, of course, that making heaven on earth isn't really possible,
and for those of us who have an understanding of what heaven is, it's just
a figure of speech for now on this sin-infected earth. But why is the phrase
meaningful to us at all? I believe it is because on earth is precisely where
we'd most like to spend forever. We get rightly excited about things we
can smell, touch, taste, hear, and see with our physical senses. When we
are told that heaven isn't really a place as much as it is a condition, a
mode of existence without sin where we'll rejoice forever, we have to really take that by faith, because, frankly, it doesn't sound very enticing.

In his book *The Journey of Desire*, John Eldredge accurately describes
the feelings many of us have as we contemplate the familiar idea of heav-
en: "We have settled on an image of the never-ending sing-along in the
sky, one great hymn after another, forever and ever, amen. And our heart
sinks. *Forever and ever? That's it? That's the good news?* And then we sigh
and feel guilty that we are not more 'spiritual.' We lose heart, and we turn
once more to the present to find what life we can."[1]

We just can't help feeling a little guilty about not being excited about
heaven, even if it were just singing hymns in the sky forever. After all, who
could ever complain about being in the presence of Jesus forever, wherever or however that might be? The answer is no true Christian would, not
for a second. Yet that isn't the issue. If that were what was promised us, we
would accept it. But it isn't. We have many mistaken ideas about heaven
that have been sabotaging our desire for the better country promised us.

- Heaven is an interminable church service that goes on forever and ever.
- Heaven is bland, colorless, and dull, an eternal form of monasticism.
- Heaven is a condition more than a place, a spiritual existence, not a physical one.
- Heavenly descriptions in Scripture are strictly symbolic.
- Heaven is unknowable, since eye has not seen, nor ear heard, nor mind conceived what God has prepared for those who love Him.
- Heaven will replace earth because earth is sinful.
- Heaven's occupants are all that is important about it.

The list goes on and on. Some of these erroneous ideas about heaven contain elements of truth. Heaven certainly will be a life of glorified character free from sin; that must not be minimized. But neither should place be minimized if that place were created by God for us to enjoy forever. And certainly there is much about heaven that is unknowable, but we can and should speak about what *has been* told us about heaven. God has not been silent on this key issue. The architect and occupant of heaven is by far the most important thing about heaven because He is the lover of our souls and our redeemer and savior, but if He has chosen a place for us to live with Him, and revealed some of it to us, isn't it likely there is a reason?

Earth Will Be Restored

I had many mistaken ideas of heaven over the years, including a number of those mentioned. Part of my misunderstanding of heaven was a result of not realizing that God had planned to restore creation from the effects of sin. Sin didn't just affect mankind, as we know, but earth and the heavens as well. As Paul wrote, "We know that the whole creation has been groaning as in the pains of childbirth right up to the present time" (Romans 8:22). Not only do *we* look forward to being liberated from the suffering sin brought into our world, but so does creation itself. "The creation itself will be liberated from its bondage to decay and brought into the glorious freedom of the children of God" (Romans 8:21).

In his book *Heaven*, Randy Alcorn writes, "It is no coincidence that the first two chapters of the Bible (Genesis 1–2) begin with the creation of the heavens and the earth and the last two chapters (Revelation 21–22) begin with the re-creation of the heavens and the earth. All that was lost at the beginning will be restored at the end. And far more will be added besides."[2]

This is not some new teaching but something that the Old Testament promised and the New Testament confirmed.

"Peter answered [Jesus], "We have left everything to follow you! What then will there be for us?"(Matthew 19:27–28). I find it interesting that Peter wanted to know what reward the disciples could expect for their faith in and service to Christ. Jesus did not rebuke him and say, "Now that's a terrible attitude to have, Peter. You shouldn't be thinking about yourself; that's selfish and very unspiritual."

Instead, Jesus felt the question was not only legitimate but also deserving of a clear answer: "Jesus said to them, 'I tell you the truth, *at the renewal of all things*, when the Son of Man sits on his glorious throne, you who have followed me will also sit on twelve thrones, judging the twelve tribes of Israel'" (emphasis added). What are the "all things" that will be renewed? Certainly we will be renewed, but there is more to "all things" than just us. Interestingly, Peter repeats this idea in his sermon in the book of Acts as he preaches to the Jews about Jesus. "He must remain in heaven," Peter tells them, "until the time comes for God to *restore everything*, as he promised long ago through his holy prophets" (Acts 3:21, emphasis added). What promises were those?

- "In the beginning you laid the foundations of the earth, and the heavens are the work of your hands. They will perish, but you remain; they will all wear out like a garment. Like clothing you will change them and they will be discarded" (Psalm 102:25, 26).
- "Behold, I will create new heavens and a new earth" (Isaiah 65:17).
- " 'As the new heavens and the new earth that I make will endure before me,' declares the Lord, 'so will your name and descendants endure' " (Isaiah 66:22).

The apostles of Jesus did not try to spiritualize those promises; they reiterated them.

> At that time his voice shook the earth, but now he has promised, "Once more I will shake not only the earth but also the heavens." The words "once more" indicate the removing of what can be shaken— that is, created things—so that what cannot be shaken may remain. Therefore, since we are receiving a kingdom that cannot be shaken, let us be thankful, and so worship God acceptably with reverence and awe, for our "God is a consuming fire" (Hebrews 12:26–29).

Peter was stubbornly convinced that this event was really going to happen.

> But the day of the Lord will come like a thief. The heavens will disappear with a roar; the elements will be destroyed by fire, and the earth and everything in it will be laid bare . . . That day will bring about the destruction of the heavens by fire, and the elements will melt in the heat. *But in keeping with his promise we are looking forward to a new heaven and a new earth, the home of righteousness*" (2 Peter 3:10–13, emphasis added).

Whose promise was this? It was Jesus' promise!

Renewal and Restoration

The apostle John received the Revelation from Jesus of this new heaven and new earth, a bold crescendo to the entire revelation of God, displaying the scene in vivid color and detail. "Then I saw a new heaven and a new earth, for the first heaven and the first earth had passed away" (Revelation 21:1). Two entire chapters are used to describe this time and place. This is the *renewal* and the *restoration* that were spoken of in Isaiah 65 and 66, Matthew 19, and Acts 3.

We often get confused about these things because we are painfully aware of the way sin has affected and infected the whole creation. Yet, it is sin that is the problem, not the creation itself. When God created the heavens and the earth, He pronounced them good. There was nothing wrong with God's original design of earth or our bodies or our universe.

He is not planning to trash the whole design, but to renew and restore it to an infinitely better than original condition.

"The power of Christ's resurrection is enough not only to remake us," Alcorn points out, "but also to remake every inch of the universe—mountains, rivers, plants, animals, stars, nebulae, quasars, and galaxies. Christ's redemptive work extends resurrection to the far reaches of the universe. This is a stunning affirmation of God's greatness. It should move our hearts to wonder and praise."[3]

One theologian, speaking of the new heavens and new earth writes, "They are called 'new,' but this does not mean new in the absolute sense; for 'the earth abideth forever' (Psalm 104:5; 119:90; Ecclesiastes 1:4)." Another theologian writes, "In those passages which speak of the passing away of the earth and heaven (Matthew 5:18, 24, 35; Mark 13:30, 31; Luke 16:17) the original word is never one which signifies termination of existence . . . That it implies great changes when applied to the earth and heavens is very evident; but that it ever means annihilation, or the passing of things *out of being* there is no clear instance either in the scriptures or in classic Greek to prove. The main idea is transition, not extinction . . . Why should it be thought a strange thing that matter is to exist forever? If God desires it to continue then all human opinion to the contrary does not count."[4]

Jesus told us in Matthew 5:5, "Blessed are the meek, for they will inherit the earth." If earth is entirely destroyed and we live somewhere in an ethereal condition, exactly when will this be fulfilled? Did Jesus really believe the crowd He was speaking to would understand this as a spiritual reference alone?

There is simply an abundance of definitive scriptural evidence that heaven is a place, a new place made out of the old earth and heavens. Against all hope (and much bad information), we learn that God is creating a new place for us to live forever that is a real, tangible, physical place. But we are often reluctant to believe we should use our present earth and the present heavens as models of what is coming.

We are told again and again that descriptions of heaven are merely spiritual. Even C. S. Lewis, one of my favorite authors and a personal hero, wrote, "There is no need to be worried by facetious people who try to make the Christian hope of 'Heaven' ridiculous by saying they do not want 'to spend eternity playing harps.' The answer to such people is that if they cannot understand books written for grown-ups, they should not talk about them. All the scriptural imagery (harps, crowns, gold, etc.) is, of course, a merely symbolical attempt to express the inexpressible . . . People who take these symbols literally might as well think that when Christ told us to be like doves, He meant that we were to lay eggs."[5]

Heavenly Symbolism or Reality?

While I agree with Lewis that there is much symbolism in the Bible, especially in descriptions of the new heavens and the new earth, I disagree with him that these symbols may never be understood literally. His implication is that something that is meant to be symbolic can't also have literal meaning as well. But is this true? Just because something has symbolic meaning doesn't mean it can't also refer to something real, or literal. In other words, symbols are often used to represent greater truths or real things. A crown is symbolic of ruling and reigning, yet it is a real thing. Monarchs today wear crowns at formal affairs, symbolizing their position within the monarchy.

Adam and Eve were to become symbolic of all people, yet they were also real human beings. The offerings in the Old Testament were symbolic of the coming sacrifice of Christ, yet they were also literal things, like lambs and doves and grain. The Old Testament temple—a real, physical place—was full of symbolic meaning. The Ark of the Covenant was a tangible object that was highly symbolic in its entire design. The book of Revelation describes real experiences and events, but these events are occasionally shrouded in symbolism.

Certainly there are times when events or things in the Bible are intended to be understood only symbolically, but in the case of the new heavens and earth, where many passages of Scripture promise a physical, tangible renewal and tell us that they will be our new home, to spiritualize this concept into meaninglessness results in misunderstanding.

Furthermore, it is clear that our ancestors in the faith understood heaven as not only perfection, but as a physical place. They were longing for a country—a city. It is tempting to spiritualize these concepts, and many do. But the point is this: would Abraham have thought of heaven as a spiritual state, or as a physical place? When Hebrews tells us that he was looking for a city—a country—Abraham would know only one kind of city, one kind of country—the earthly kind. He was definitely looking for a better country, a heavenly one, but what he was expecting would be countryish, tangible.

Renewed or Recreated?

Many Christians are more excited about the millennial reign of Christ spoken of in Isaiah 65 and other places in Scripture than they are of their ideas of ultimate heaven. The reason is that the scriptural descriptions of the millennial kingdom are so earthly and familiar—and yet so much *better by far* than our present earthly condition. But even that amazing earthly kingdom will be destroyed to make way for the better country!

We are not only made *for* earth but made *out of* earth. If we were not destined to live in a physical place, we would no longer need physical bodies with legs to walk upon surfaces and eyes to see things with and mouths to speak with. Furthermore, God took great pains to put His people in a very specific land—the Promised Land. If spiritual realities always trump physical ones, all God's past, present, and future promises to the nation of Israel don't make a lot of sense.

Will new heavens and new earth be exactly like old heavens and old earth? No, it is quite clear that old earth and old heavens will be destroyed. But will new heavens and new earth be completely different—will they be made in a completely new mold? I believe not. They will be a *new* earth and a *new* heaven, but they will be an earth and a heaven. God never said He was going to get rid of the earthly and heavenly realities with which we are familiar. The very words *earth, heaven,* and *body* carry specific meanings for us, and God knows that.

Is earth renewed, or entirely recreated? *To renew* or *regenerate* is to take something familiar and change it so that it is in one sense new and yet, in another sense, familiar to its original form. To be born again is called regeneration. Paul reminds us in 2 Corinthians 5:17 that regeneration consists of old things passing away but also new things coming. Are we made new in Christ? Absolutely. Yet are we now, and will we in the future, still be human and resemble our old selves? Yes—Jesus in His resurrected body was recognizable as the old Jesus—yet better by far! Both familiar and new are joined together in a profound "renewal."

It would have been easy for God to merely say, "I will destroy heaven and earth and your bodies and make something brand new." Yet when He speaks of what is coming, he uses terms of familiarity.

When the disciples first saw Jesus after His resurrection, some thought He was a ghost or a spirit, assuming that the physical body is something to cast off at death as no longer important. But it was Jesus who corrected this idea from the beginning by inviting the disciples to "Look at my hands and my feet. It is I myself! Touch me and see; a ghost does not have flesh and bones, as you see I have." When he had said this, he showed them his hands and feet" (Luke 24:39–40).

Were we to share the disciples' assumptions about our glorified bodies after our resurrection, we would simply say that they aren't bodies at all. After all, who needs bodies in heaven if heaven is indeed more a state or condition than a place? Yet orthodox Christianity confirms that we will be raised with physical bodies, bodies like our risen Lord's that was physical, tangible, and observable—real bodies.

Why will we need to have a resurrected body with flesh and bones if we will be living in an ethereal world? Jesus restored His human body, as He will restore ours. Our bodies will be different, as His is, better by far—but *bodies*, nonetheless. Jesus will return not only to complete the redemption of mankind but also of the whole creation.

The great Christmas truth is that God became the God/Man: a physical man—a real 24/7, genuine, "like-the-rest-of-us" man—except without sin. Why would He do that—and connect Himself *eternally* to this human form—unless He knew He'd be fitting Himself to reign forever on a new, tangible, physical earth? He could have taken on human form for a while—just long enough to complete our redemption. But this divine incarnation connects the fall in Eden in Genesis to the new earth of Revelation. It is on a new earth that Christ will ultimately reign forever—in an earthly glorified body. Earth was not just a grand experiment that went awry; it was, and is, His eternal plan for us.

It is a popular idea that somehow it is more spiritual to think of heaven primarily in connection with our new character and the removal of our sin nature rather than to think of a physical place we might live forever.

Of course, there is much truth in this. The most perfect place would be devastated and completely unenjoyable with our current sin natures— Eden proved that.

Yet when Adam and Eve were created in the garden, they were in a state of what theologians often term "untested creaturely holiness." They had (at the time) perfectly holy character, and yet God prepared an incredible physical world for them to live in. Mountains, rivers, trees, animals, foods, smells, and sights were all part of God's idea. But where did God choose to reside? He enjoyed walking with man in the garden! Place, as unspiritual as it may sound to some, is very important to God. It is part of His plan not only for us—but for Himself as well.

We look forward to heaven *most* because we will be with Him and like Him forever, yet our eternal lives will be lived out in the new earth and the new heavens; that is part of our inheritance, the part that Adam originally squandered. We will get it back.

Lifeboat to Ark Theology

Paul Marshall, in his book *Heaven Is Not My Home: Learning to Live in God's Creation*, describes what he sees as the problem with popular conceptions of heaven. He suggests that many modern Christians have the erroneous view that somehow our world is "wrecked," and what's important is that we rescue people from the wreckage. Marshall calls this view "lifeboat theology." He likens creation to the Titanic, and now that humanity has hit the iceberg of sin, there's nothing left but to get everyone into lifeboats. The ship (earth) is sinking, and the only thing God is concerned with is getting people off the boat before it goes down.

Marshall proposes an alternative to lifeboat theology that he calls ark theology. When God decided to destroy the earth the first time with water, He didn't annihilate the earth. God's people and selected animals were saved; only that which God wanted to get rid of was destroyed. After the flood had subsided, Noah took up residence on the same earth God had earlier judged and was commanded to be fruitful. God judged the earth with water the first time (the term *destroyed* was used); the next time it will be "destroyed" with fire. But earth is destined to be renewed, made new—for us.

There are those who would say that we were just being materialists by describing heaven in physical, material ways. Heaven, we are reminded, is spiritual. Yes, but so am I, and I am also physical. When I receive my glorified, resurrected body I will be both spiritual and tangible (observable, real). The two are not in contradiction with each other but rather are complimentary. Paul tells us in 1 Corinthians 15 that a person's body will be raised imperishable, because while "it is sown in dishonor, it is raised in glory; it is sown in weakness, it is raised in power; it is sown a natural body, it is raised a spiritual body" (1 Corinthians 15:43–44). But Paul makes it clear that our bodies will be like our Lord's resurrected body. Our Lord's resurrected body is the first fruits; our bodies will be raised when He comes.

While our Lord's body was raised imperishable, it was tangible. A spiritual body does not mean an intangible body. Jesus' body was able to touch, feel, eat, and interact with a physical planet with ease. Human beings could see it, touch it, talk with it, and embrace it. It is spiritual precisely because it is imperishable, immortal, powerful rather than weak, and glorified rather than humiliated. Our spiritual body will be a tangible body. There is no such thing as a non-physical body. You can have a non-physical form, but not a non-physical body.

Theologian Louis Berkhof writes, "Many conceive of heaven also as a subjective condition, which men may enjoy in the present and which in the way of righteousness will naturally become permanent in the future . . . But we should not think of the joys of heaven, however, as exclusively spiritual. There will be something corresponding to the body. There will be recognition and social intercourse on an elevated plane."[6]

Heaven on Earth: Both Familiar and New

Randy Alcorn suggests that too often we spiritualize the words *city, country,* or *body:*

"For example, we're told that Heaven is a city (Hebrews 11:10; 13:14). When we hear the word city, we shouldn't scratch our heads and think, 'I wonder what that means?' We understand cities. Cities have buildings, culture, art, music, athletics, goods and services, events of all kinds. And, of course, cities have people engaged in activities, gatherings, conversations and work. Heaven is also described as a country (Hebrews 11:16). We know about countries. They have territories, rulers, national interests, pride in their identity, and citizens who are both diverse and unified.

"If we can't imagine our present Earth without rivers, mountains, trees, and flowers, then why would we try to imagine the New Earth without these features? We wouldn't expect a non-Earth to have mountains and rivers. But God doesn't promise us a non-Earth. He promises us a New Earth. If the word Earth in this phrase means anything, it means that we can expect to find earthly things there—including atmosphere, mountains, water, trees, people, houses—even cities, buildings and streets. These familiar features are specifically mentioned in Revelation 21–22."[7]

We often hear the familiar refrain that to ascribe any idea to heaven is hopeless, because as Paul reminds us in 1 Corinthians 2:9, "No eye has seen, no ear has heard, no mind has conceived what God has prepared for those who love him." It is fruitless to try to imagine anything about heaven, we are told, because it is impossible. And on the surface, that is true. To try to imagine heaven is futile. Unless heaven, or at least some information about it, is revealed to us, we are clueless. Yet the next verse reminds us "but God has revealed it to us by his Spirit" (1 Corinthians 2:10).

We must be so careful not to go beyond what God has revealed. There are things that God has no intention of revealing to us now about many things (including heaven). Remember, Paul, in 2 Corinthians 12, was forbidden to speak about what he had seen and heard in paradise. Deuteronomy 29:29 reminds us, "The secret things belong to the Lord our God, but the things revealed belong to us and to our children forever." Yet it is just as wrong to ignore what God has told us, as it is to go beyond what He has told us.

The Importance of Place

Place, as much as we might find it hard to believe, is important to God. It is part of His creation—the part for us. Eden wasn't just fellowship with God; it was a real, tangible place. Israel, the Promised Land, wasn't just a spiritual truth or ideal; it was a genuine piece of real estate, a promised place. The temple of God where God's presence dwelt was a tangible, localized place where God chose to make Himself visible to us (or reveal Himself to us). Our resurrected bodies will be eternally united with our perfected spirits. We won't be disembodied spirits floating around an ethereal city. The Bible records over and over the importance of place—Israel, the temple, Jerusalem, Bethlehem, Nazareth, the plains of Megiddo, and on and on.

Heaven is referred to as a city or a country—in other words, a place. Heaven will be that final and eternal experience where perfection of person and perfection of place finally join together forever.

But having said all that, it is important to remember that the Bible teaches that the new heavens and new earth will not commence until the very end, after the rapture, after Christ comes again, after the millennial period, the resurrection, and the great white throne judgment (Revelation 20–21). If you think about this, you will see that this leaves us with a period of time between our passing from this life to the next, and that final state. Since we'll no longer be on earth or in our old bodies and won't yet be on the new earth in our resurrected bodies, where exactly do believers go when they die, and what are they like in this place?

We'll be in the same place that Abraham, Moses, David, the disciples, and every true believer in God who has died lives now. We'll join the repentant thief on the cross as well as all our loved ones in the faith—in paradise.

We won't be in the better country yet, but we will definitely be in a better place by far, a place of inexpressible joy in the presence of our Lord and Savior. A place of awareness and activity. What exactly will that be like?

The journey continues.

CHAPTER FOUR

Waking Up in Heaven

Jesus answered him, "I tell you the truth, today you will be with me in paradise" (LUKE 23:43).

One day, maybe not for a while, but someday Dan Schaeffer will breathe his last breath. It is that moment that so many people dread—that moment when our greatest fears and our deepest faith will collide. My last glimpse of life on this earth will have been experienced, and all of what I had known as earth will be lost to sight, though not to memory. The moment of my last earthly exhalation will be my first moment of eternal inhalation; I will breathe, ironically, for the last time mortally and first time eternally simultaneously. Faith shall finally become sight.

Then . . . *paradise!*

Seeing my risen Lord! Reunion! Rejoicing! Marveling!

The beginning of *forever*.

No longer will I see dimly as through a glass. Paradise will be a sight and a sound and a feel and a place I could never have imagined on earth. And the amazing part is that this is not yet the better country we are waiting for. It will be the most beautiful, glorious, enchanting, holy, and perfect experience we could ever hope for. It will not yet, ironically, be our eternal home, but it will be in every conceivable way . . . *paradise!*

It surprises some people to learn that upon our death none of us go either to heaven or to hell. It is only at the end of time, at the great white throne judgment, that this will take place. Only then do we inherit and enter the better country, and those who have rejected mercy and grace receive their final judgment (Revelation 20–21). In fact, the new earth won't be created until that time, so it would be impossible to go there upon our death. There is, obviously, a prolonged period of time when the current events of history must play themselves out upon this earthly stage and all prophecy be fulfilled. Our loved ones in Christ, who have gone on before us, are now waiting for that same thing. But where?

Pre–Heaven

What happens the moment after we die is what most people really want to know. Where do we go? What will it be like? Who will be there? Will I be aware of my surroundings? What form will I have? How will I get there? Who will I see? What will I do? These questions are the most immediate for us, and fortunately, we do have information provided us by the Scriptures.

While many theologians call this interim period "intermediate heaven," and that is for all intents and purposes an adequate description, I fear it leaves us with the wrong idea: that we really aren't going to heaven when we die. Technically, we can state that the better country won't be completely ready (or open) to us until after the end of all human history and the earth and the heavens are made new, but surely paradise, as Jesus called it, is the first great experience of true heaven for us. Many aspects of final heaven will be there, including the presence of our Lord, the presence of our loved ones in Christ, and the presence of the angels. There will be rejoicing, gladness, peace, wonder, and consciousness we've never known. As a result, I prefer the term pre-heaven to intermediate heaven.

Pre-heaven is not simply a stopgap, a really nice holding tank; it is paradise itself. It is where the saints of the Old Testament and all those who have died in Christ have existed since their earthly passing.

The term *pre-heaven* presupposes that our next destination has many of the features we long for in the better country, and I believe that to be the case. We know that we will be with Christ (Luke 23:29–43; 2 Corinthians 5:6–8; 2 Corinthians 12:4; Revelation 2:7) in what is called paradise. Is that a place? Surely. Jesus is *somewhere* in His glorified physical body, not *everywhere*. This does not diminish His omnipresence (being everywhere present), but His body, being human, is localized. His body is a glorified *human* body, a tangible body that was designed for earthly living, hence the need for legs to walk upon the earth, arms to gather and touch and feel, eyes to see what there is to see, ears to hear what there is to hear, a nose to smell with, a mouth to talk and eat with. All those aspects of His physical body exist now and will exist forever. Though He is not on the new earth, He is in a place. It may be a place unlike anything we could possibly conceive of, but a place nonetheless.

Where He is, that's where we'll be. Absent from the body is to be present with the Lord. We will be in paradise.

From Earth to Paradise

In Luke 23, when Jesus was dying on the cross between two thieves, one repented of his deeds at the end and cried out for mercy from our Lord. "Then he said, 'Jesus, remember me when you come into your kingdom.' Jesus answered him, 'I tell you the truth, today you will be with me in paradise'" (Luke 23:42–43).

Paradise is a word of Persian origin and means a garden, particularly a garden of pleasure, filled with trees, shrubs, fountains, and flowers. God created a paradise in Eden, lush and beautiful, and the Hebrew word for Eden was often used in the Old Testament to describe fertile pleasant places as a translation of the word *garden*. In the hot Palestinian climate, gardens were especially important and pleasant, and that is why the rich and powerful often had lavish gardens. So the word *paradise* ultimately came to mean a place of happiness and was particularly used to describe the home of the blessed in the next life. It speaks of the presence of God, His dwelling place, so it doesn't really mean that it is an intermediate place. It might be a temporary place *for us* after we die and before new earth and new heavens are created, but it is His home, His presence, and always has been.

In the Old Testament, all people who died were said to go to Sheol, the place of departed spirits, both believers and non-believers alike. There was within Sheol two divisions, one for believers, and one for unbelievers. One was paradise, or Abraham's bosom; the other was the place of judgment. In the New Testament, *Hades* is the transliteration of the Hebrew word *Sheol* and came to be used exclusively for the place of judgment. Gehenna was another term Jesus used, the place of unquenchable fires. Hell is the word we use, but it refers to the same Hades or Gehenna, the place of judgment. Hades, right now, is not the final hell, as paradise is not the final heaven. But each has distinct characteristics of its ultimate counterparts.

In the New Testament, the word *paradise* (*paradeisos*) is used only three times, each time to signify a place of exquisite pleasure and delight (Luke 23:43; 2 Corinthians 12:4; Revelation 2:7). Paul makes it clear in 2 Corinthians 12:2 and 4 that paradise is the same as the third heaven. The apostle Paul had been to the third heaven, or paradise, in the presence of Christ, either in spirit or transported physically in some way he didn't understand. In fact, the apostle Paul is one of only two humans who has ever been taken to see paradise and returned to tell about it (the other is the apostle John), although he was not able to say much. He heard "inexpressible things, things that a man is not permitted to tell" (2 Corinthians 12:4).

How much did this affect Paul? Paul would go on to suffer as possibly no other apostle had suffered; he would face distress, persecution, beatings, shipwreck, and many other calamities. It appears that in light of what Paul would have to face in life, God allowed him a special vision, a glimpse of heaven that would be seared into his memory forever. In those moments of distress he would be able to continue on, so certain of what lay before him that he could endure his earthly suffering. But at the same time, this vision he had of heaven would cause him to desire to return. He confessed to the Philippian church his struggle: "If I am to go on living in the body, this will mean fruitful labor for me. Yet what shall I choose? I do not know! I am torn between the two: *I desire to depart and be with Christ, which is better by far*; but it is more necessary for you that I remain in the body" (Philippians 1:22–24, emphasis added).

We can all infer that being in the presence of our Lord in paradise would be wonderful beyond words, but Paul alone could say with authority, "It is *better by far*!" For us, we take it by faith. For Paul, it was an experience he had already had, a place he had been, the memory fueling his difficult and painful ministry for Christ. We don't know if he saw all there was to see of paradise, or just a glimpse of it. Either way, the impression left upon him was permanent. Nothing on earth could ever satisfy him the same way again.

Paul knew all about this life. He knew all the pleasures that could be had here. He had witnessed the beauty our earth has to offer, the joy of human relationships, and the pleasant experiences we can have on earth. Yet paradise was *better by far*! Let that sink in. Before we ever reach our final destination, which will be more amazing than anything we can imagine, we will be in paradise, which is also more amazing than anything we can imagine. We must not, for a moment, regret the time we will be in paradise as wasted or a disappointment, because it is not yet our final home. In the presence of our Lord, we are at home, whether in paradise or the new heavens and new earth. In the presence of our Lord, there is joy, gladness, and peace.

What Can We Learn of Paradise?

Do we have any biblical information on this paradise, any clues as to what we might be able to expect? Yes. Before Jesus ever hung on the cross, He spoke to His disciples and the Pharisees in Luke 16. Jesus reminded them of the importance of being "welcomed into eternal dwellings" (Luke 16:9). Later He says, "If you have not been trustworthy with someone else's property, who will give you property of your own?" (Luke 16:11). The riches He was referring to were heavenly riches.

Then, Jesus told a story (not a parable—indicating this was an actual experience) about a rich man who lived in luxury every day (Luke 16:19–31). At the rich man's gate laid a beggar named Lazarus who was covered with sores and longed to eat what fell from the rich man's table. Things were so bad the dogs came and licked his sores, a painful and humiliating experience. But the time came when the beggar died, and the angels came and carried him to Abraham's side (or "bosom" in many versions). The Jews believed that the spirits of righteous men were taken to heaven by angels at their death, and Jesus confirms this idea here. Abraham's side, or Abraham's bosom, is a phrase taken from the Jewish practice of reclining at meals, when the head of one person lay on the side or chest of another. Over time the phrase came to describe intimacy and friendship. Since all the Jews knew that Abraham was in paradise, to say that Lazarus was at Abraham's side was the same as saying he was in paradise. Lazarus had been admitted to paradise, but the rich man had not.

The rich man, we are told, was in hell (Hades), where he was in torment but was able to see Abraham far away with Lazarus by his side. He begs Abraham to have pity and send Lazarus to dip his finger in water and cool his tongue to relieve some of his agony. But Abraham told him this was impossible because both Lazarus and he were receiving their just rewards for their lives; besides, there was a fixed chasm that separated paradise from Hades that could not be breached.

Our Lord, having experienced paradise and Hades firsthand, would certainly know the details of both. First, we notice that both the saved and the condemned are conscious and aware of their surroundings and condition. We can also see that in some way, Lazarus was instantly recognizable as Lazarus to the rich man. The rich man saw Lazarus and recognized him from afar. We also can surmise that our souls have features that are similar in some ways to our bodies , because the rich man asked Lazarus to dip his finger into some water to cool his own tongue. Obviously Lazarus' and the rich man's bodies were still on earth in various forms of decay, yet this passage seems to indicate physicality of some sort. That the rich man could speak and Abraham and Lazarus could hear is also stated, again indications of tangible bodily forms—ears and mouths—to hear and make sound.

One of the most important questions we have is if we will exist in paradise, or pre-heaven, as disembodied spirits. This is an important question for us who are presently physical beings and whose destiny it is to have glorified physical bodies.

Berkhof, a renowned theologian, writes, "Many conceive of heaven also as a subjective condition, which men may enjoy in the present and which in the way of righteousness will naturally become permanent in the future. But here, too, it must be said that Scripture clearly presents heaven as a place. Christ *ascended* to heaven, which can only mean that He went from one place to another. It is described as the house of our Father with many mansions, John 14:1, and this description would hardly fit a condition. Moreover, believers are said to be within, while unbelievers are without (Matthew 22:12, 13; 25:10–12). Scripture gives us reasons to believe that the righteous will not only inherit heaven, but the entire new creation, Matthew 5:5, Revelation 21:1–3 . . . We should not think of the joys of heaven, however, as exclusively spiritual."[1]

When Jesus told the thief that he would be with Him this day in paradise, it is acknowledged that it would have to be in some "soulish" way, because their physical bodies would still be in their graves that day. This is why some theologians have speculated that we might have some form of soulish bodies or temporary physical or tangible forms of some kind to live in during our time in paradise prior to receiving our glorified bodies at the resurrection at the end of time. Furthermore, it appears we are recognizable as the person we were before.

There is discussion about what Paul means in 2 Corinthians, where the apostle wrote to the church at Corinth about our eternal future: "Now we know that if the earthly tent we live in is destroyed, we have a building from God, an eternal house in heaven, not built by human hands" (2 Corinthians 5:1).

The question is what period is Paul referring to here: the pre-heaven paradise or the future resurrection? It is difficult to be certain, so we must be careful, but Paul does seem to be indicating that the human soul desires to be found clothed and not naked, suggesting a time of existence without a body.

This would help explain the presence of Moses and Elijah, who appeared with Jesus on the Mount of Transfiguration. In Luke 9:28–36, we read that when Jesus was transfigured before Peter, James, and John, Moses and Elijah appeared in "glorious splendor." It is important to note that these two spiritual luminaries were recognizable as human beings, glorious human beings. Moses and Elijah were citizens of paradise. While Elijah had been taken to heaven without dying (2 Kings 2:1, 11–12), Moses had died (Deuteronomy 34:5–8). Yet both were visible with bodies that appeared human. How else would the disciples have recognized them as men?

In Revelation 6, we read of the opening of the fifth seal, and we are shown the souls of those who had been slain, the martyrs of the church of Jesus Christ. They call out to our Lord and ask, "How long, Sovereign Lord, holy and true, until you judge the inhabitants of the earth and avenge our blood?" (Revelation 6:10). Then the Lord gave each of them a white robe, and they were told to wait a little longer. Again, we find people in paradise, pre-heaven, who are conscious, aware of their surroundings, and even more, aware of the events that are occurring on earth below. They are clothed with robes of white. There must be some form to clothe if they are clothed with robes. They have voices to cry out with to God, meaning they have some way to communicate verbally.

There appears to be some bodily form, though not the physical kind we are used to, available to saints in paradise. It is also clear that we will be conscious and aware of what is happening around us, and even a little, at least, of what is happening on earth. That makes sense. We know that the angels are spectators of the earthly drama, and we have far more invested in what happens on earth than do the angels. It would be reasonable that we would be able to know or see what is happening with those we most care about.

Though the Bible does not teach that we can or should pray to those who have gone before us into heaven—we are told to pray to God alone—it might be possible for them, if they are observing what is going on below, to pray to the Lord for us.

Will we join the "great cloud of witnesses" spoken of in Hebrews 12:1? It is certainly possible. We won't just be wandering and waiting in heaven, spending endless years of boredom in heavenly loitering. That would hardly fit the description of "better by far" than earth. In paradise there is both angelic and divine activity, and certainly we will also be active.

It seems only reasonable that we will be captivated by the final scenes being played out on earth below, while interacting with those with whom we have been reunited, as well as those who are our heroes in the faith (David, Moses, John the Baptist, Paul, Peter, James, and John, for example). We will be in the continual presence of our Lord, which is joy unspeakable itself, and amazed, I'm sure, at the angelic activity going on. There will be no sitting on clouds and no boring ethereal activities. Whatever we will be observing will be far more fascinating than anything Hollywood could dream up.

What Can I Expect the Moment after I Die?

As I shared earlier, one day I will finally give up my earthly life and die. At that moment, what can I expect? It appears that I will be instantly in the presence of angels (or an angel), who will usher me into the presence of my Lord Jesus. That is what Jesus said in his story of Lazarus and the rich man and what Hebrews 1:14 seems to indicate: "Are not all angels ministering spirits sent to serve those who will inherit salvation?" (Hebrews 1:14).

I think that most likely, these will be angels who will know me well, probably who have come to my rescue at the direction of our Lord numerous times. They will be the first ones, probably, who welcome or escort me into paradise. It will not be a fearful meeting, as meetings with angels in the Old Testament often were. I will no longer fear death or pain or danger; those things have passed. There will be gladness and joy and celebration in this angelic escort.

Maybe only then will I begin to understand how often I have been in unrecognized danger and rescued. Maybe the angels will share these things with us; maybe we won't even be interested in the topic. Though I am sure they will know me well, I will not know them. There are some authorities on heaven that suggest that even now we could begin to "talk" to our guardian angels (since we know they are around). Again, the Bible makes it clear that we are to pray to our Lord alone. Though it is certain that we are in the presence of angels we can't see, who are working on our behalf, it is speculation that just one is "assigned" to us.

In any event, my first sight in my new life might well be an angelic being or even paradise itself in the presence of many angels. While that may sound exciting, I know I will be anxious to see my Lord. It is His presence I crave, not an angel's. But I'm convinced that angels will bring me (and you, if you are a child of God) directly to my Lord's presence. Remember, Jesus became a man with a glorified human body upon His resurrection. He will be *some* place, not *every* place. Though God is spirit (John 4:24), He has also taken on human form. He still exists fully as God, not losing His omnipresence, but choosing to remain visible and tangibly physical in a specific locality, even while He is everywhere present in spirit. Jesus abides in paradise physically.

I will be brought to Him, and I will see Him as He is, and it will be paradise! The importance of place will fade away in His presence. I will be reunited with those I love and who have gone before me in the Lord as Lazarus was with Abraham. In some way I will have, I believe, a tangible form or body of some kind. It will at least appear human. I will recognize others (by sight possibly). More importantly, I will be Dan. I will have my same personality (improved and perfected), feelings, and thoughts (again, improved and perfected). I will know not only who I am but also who I was before.

Anecdotal Confirmation of Scriptural Teaching

While it appears to be the teaching of Scripture that we will have human form of some kind, there is also ample anecdotal evidence as well. Even though there are many, many anecdotal experiences we could share here, as convincing as they seem to be, we must remember they do not carry the authority of Scripture. They can be used, however, to support what Scripture affirms. Both believers and non-believers on their deathbeds report seeing visions and sights that are "seeable," that is, familiar faces, places, and surroundings. Erwin Lutzer relates the following story in his book *One Minute after You Die*:

"Judson B. Palmer relates the story of the Reverend A. D. Sandborn, who preceded him as pastor in a church in Iowa. Reverend Sandborn called on a young Christian woman who was seriously ill. She was bolstered up in bed, almost in a sitting position, looking off in the distance. 'Now just as soon as they open the gate I will go in,' she whispered.

"Then she sank upon her pillow in disappointment. 'They have let Mamie go in ahead of me, but soon I will go in.'

"Moments later she again spoke. 'They let Grampa in ahead of me, but next time I will go in for sure.'

"No one spoke to her and she said nothing more to anyone, and seemed to see nothing except the sights of the beautiful city. Reverend Sandborn then left the house because of the press of other duties.

"Later in the day the pastor learned that the young woman had died that morning. He was so impressed with what she had said that he asked the family about the identity of Mamie and Grampa. Mamie was a little girl who had lived near them at one time but later moved to New York State. As for Grampa, he was a friend of the family and had moved somewhere in the Southwest.

"Reverend Sandborn then wrote to the addresses given him to inquire about these two individuals. Much to his astonishment he discovered that both Mamie and Grampa had died the morning of September 16, the very hour that the young woman herself had passed into glory.' "[2]

His family gathered around him upon his deathbed, the great American evangelist, Dwight L. Moody, was quoted as saying the following: "If this is death, there is no valley. This is glorious. I have been within the gates and I saw the children, Dwight and Irene [his two grandchildren who had preceded him in death]. Earth is receding. Heaven is approaching. God is calling me."

More recently, in the bestselling book *90 Minutes in Heaven*, Pastor Don Piper details the horrific automobile accident in which he was involved and his subsequent death pronouncement on the scene by medical personnel. He then goes on to describe his arrival in heaven and the next ninety minutes he claims to have spent there. Though he survived the accident, the memories of his experience left him changed forever. His account is compelling and his descriptions consistent with what you would expect based on what we learn in Scripture, although there are still those who question the validity of Piper's experience. Whatever we conclude about what actually happened during Piper's ninety minutes, we must remember that his descriptions do not carry the authority of Scripture itself.

Waking up in heaven for us believers will be the greatest moment we've ever experienced. For the first time we will experience life the way it was meant to be experienced, with peace of mind, understanding, comprehension, excitement, joy, and wonder. How could it be any different? We will be in His presence. No longer will faith be without sight.

Where Is Paradise Now?

The heavenly Jerusalem is spoken of as "the city of the living God. You have come to thousands upon thousands of angels in joyful assembly, to the church of the firstborn, whose names are written in heaven" (Hebrews 12:22–23). Where is this city right now? Who is in it? What is it like? As far as we can tell, this New Jerusalem that will come down out of heaven is in paradise, God's abode (read about it in Revelation 21). If this physical city with its beautiful adornments is a place when it descends to the new earth, why isn't it a place now? And who would live there besides the people and the angels of God?

Is this a place within our universe? Is it in another "spiritual" universe? We can't know, and the only time we will be concerned about it is right now. At the moment we enter it, we won't be concerned about geography.

We will be overwhelmingly reminded that the word *paradise* was accurate. Heavenly activity will be swirling around us, angelic beings populating much of paradise, mingling with the saints of God. Music, color, sights, and sounds will combine to make perfection, His abode, and our new home. We will embrace those who we had to say good-bye to with tears and sorrow. We will begin to understand many experiences and events that were so confusing on earth. We will finally really realize that our life on earth was but a drop in the oceans of eternity. We will breathe the air of paradise, and upon being taken to our home, the place we will live, we will truly begin to live happily ever after.

And if that weren't enough, the best is still to come. Remember, this is just pre-heaven, paradise. The ultimate paradise, the new heavens and the new earth, have yet to be created by God.

In *The Last Battle*, by C. S. Lewis, Aslan (who represents Christ) is speaking to the children in the last chapter, "Farewell to Shadowlands."

" 'You do not yet look so happy as I mean you to be.'

"Lucy said, 'We're so afraid of being sent away, Aslan. And you have sent us back into our world so often.'

" 'No fear of that,' said Aslan. 'Have you not guessed?'

"Their hearts leaped and a wild hope rose within them.

" 'There was a real railway accident,' said Aslan softly. 'Your father and mother and all of you are—as you used to call it in the Shadow-lands—dead. The term is over: the Holidays have begun. The dream is ended: This is the morning.' And as he spoke he no longer looked to them like a lion; but the things that began to happen after that were so great and beautiful that I cannot write them. And for us this is the end of all the stories, and we can most truly say that they all lived happily ever after. But for them it was only the beginning of the real story. All their life in this world and all their adventures in Narnia had only been the cover and the title page: now at last they were beginning Chapter One of the Great Story, which no one on earth has read: which goes on forever: in which every chapter is better than the one before."[3]

When we wake up in paradise, we will have left behind the Shadow-lands. For us, Chapter One of the Great Story will just be beginning, an adventure that will never end, each experience better than the last. For us who still live in the Shadowlands, paradise is nearer to us every day. Moment by moment it draws closer.

When the perishable has been clothed with the imperishable, and the mortal with immortality, then the saying that is written will come true: "Death has been swallowed up in victory."

"Where, O death, is your victory?

Where, O death, is your sting?" (1 Corinthians 15:54–55).

Where indeed?

"We think we are in the land of the living going to the land of the dying when in reality we are in the land of the dying going to the land of the living."[4]

The journey continues.

CHAPTER FIVE

Our Heavenly Acre

In my Father's house are many rooms; . . . I am going there to prepare a place for you (John 14:2).

We are confident, I say, and would prefer to be away from the body and *at home* with the Lord (2 Corinthians 5:8, emphasis added).

Not long ago, while we were visiting some friends up north, we all decided to go on a tour of model homes so elegant that you had to pay to enter. These weren't your ordinary model homes; these were called dream homes—and for a reason! Situated high in the Sacramento foothills, they are surrounded by pines and oaks and overlook a beautiful Alpine lake. The starting cost of the homes was over one million dollars.

These houses had been decorated to the hilt, and each kitchen had at least two refrigerators (industrial size, of course, with designer panels), cooking islands that you could dance on, at least two to three sinks, and a plasma TV. In fact, almost every room seemed to have a plasma TV in it. The bedroom mirror of one room displayed the current news! Each of these homes had an "entertainment room," which consisted of at least six oversized theater seats and a wall-size screen. The room was decorated like a movie theater, of course.

The rooms were huge and luxurious; the designer bathrooms were equipped with large Jacuzzi tubs, while the backyards sported custom pools with a designer built-in cabana for outdoor cooking and living. My favorite model of the four was the Geronimo. When you walked inside, the first thing you saw was a wall of large windows looking down upon the beautiful scene below, with distressed wood floors and a large rock wall fireplace. I have to confess that I coveted that home.

But as nice as these houses were, they are already growing old, their appliances and plumbing will eventually wear out, the paint will peel and fade, and gradually the house will give way to the ravages of time and wear. The houses were beautiful, but I would be lying if I called them home. Home is far more than just a beautiful house.

Home.

The place I belong. The place I am known. The place I want to return to over and over again.

It is such a precious word. It means so many things all at once: family, friends, buildings, rooms, familiarity, love, belonging, security, roots, and memories. There is no other word exactly like it. Home is a place of retreat, comfort, and security, where we enjoy special relationships with family. Fond memories, sights, sounds, and smells remind us we are home, and, when we are away from it, make us long to return.

Earthly Homes Can Be Broken

Sadly, not all of our memories of home are the stuff of Thomas Kinkade paintings. On earth houses can be burned up, blown away, torn down, and flooded, and our homes can be destroyed by divorce, anger, lies, and hostility—but as bad as it can be, we find that we still long for it.

I experienced three broken homes by the time I was sixteen years old. Home was often a tense, difficult, lonely, and despairing place. Yet, for all that, it was home—my home. Jane Austen wrote, "One does not love a place the less for having suffered in it."[1] I remember being terribly homesick when I was a young boy and sent away to a summer camp. Being in a strange place with strange and often unfriendly kids prompted me to find a counselor and blurt out in tears, "I want to go home." Those moments when my home was peaceful, happy, and safe had left their indelible imprint. I was homesick. I yearned to return to the place I knew and understood and felt safe. Even those who have never known a warm and endearing home life yearn for it. It is simply in every human's emotional DNA.

In heaven we will finally be home the way we've always desired it—forever.

The sense of perfect comfort, belonging, and loving that means home will finally be real. In truth, home is more an idea than a reality on earth, for it is transient and elusive. As strange as it may sound, everyone will experience a broken home, for homes cannot endure in this world. As good as your home may be, it is slowly dissolving. Children grow up and move away, spouses and loved ones age and die eventually, and our dearest earthly possessions are often left to those who see them only for their monetary value.

Home includes certain experiences that can't be repeated (the birth of our children, for example), relationships with our family change over time—we change over time. We change emotionally, physically, intellectually, and in many other ways, so that it is impossible to recapture those treasured experiences of the past that we think of when we think of home.

All we are left with at the end are faded memories. If we think about it, our dearest memories of home are nothing more than snapshots, precious moments and memories captured briefly before the tide of time washes all evidence of them away. We try to preserve our ideas of home with pictures of people and events, but even they fade with time as those who were truly moved by them leave the earthly scene.

I am reminded of old photographs I've seen from the 1800s that are in history books. I can never help wondering who the person was, why the picture was taken, who his or her family was, and what this picture might have meant at one time to someone. Over the years, all the people for whom that picture has emotional value have passed away. Yet I know that at one time it was probably a treasured family memento—a reminder to someone of family, of love, of home—a home that is no more.

Home on earth was never meant to be more than a shadow of our eternal home in heaven, because at its best, it cannot completely fulfill its promise to us. We are always left wanting more, hoping for more out of home, watching sadly as what we cared for most is slowly taken from us. As C. S. Lewis poignantly asked, "Has this world been so kind to you that you would leave it with regret? There are better things ahead than any we leave behind."[2]

We desire, at the deepest level, a home that can't change, that *won't* change. We want to be surrounded by places and people that fill us with constant joy and comfort and security forever. Our present homes can never fulfill that desire—but the one waiting for us can.

A Home Built Just for You

Jesus reminded us in John 14 that He is going to prepare a place for us. "In my Father's house are many rooms; if it were not so, I would have told you. I am going there to prepare a place for you. And if I go and prepare a place for you, I will come back and take you to be with me that you also may be where I am" (John 14:2–3).

"The mission of Christ," writes Joe Stowell, "was never intended to culminate at the cross. The cross and the empty grave were merely a means to kick the door of heaven open for us so that we could go home to be with Him. Home is where you feel comfortable, secure, safe, and at peace. In a very real sense, Jesus Christ had become the disciples' home away from home. As long as they were with Him, they felt at home. That is exactly why they were so traumatized when He told them that He was leaving them (John 13, 14)."[3]

Jesus speaks not only of heaven in a general sense—but also our heavenly acre. Not just the home of all who believe, but also *your* home. Think about it: Jesus has gone to prepare a home for *you*.

Your home.

This is important, because even here on earth, home is different for every person, even for people within the same family. Family members will have different experiences of what home means to them and how they have experienced the same home. Two people in the same family can have polar opposite ideas and memories of home. For one, home was wonderful, for another it was terrible.

Each person is incredibly unique—made that way by God Himself—so each person's home will need to be equally unique, to truly be home *to him or her*. The exciting part of going home to heaven is that God won't make a "one-size-fits-all" home for us. I believe your home will be different from all others in specific ways because you are different from all others in specific ways.

In *The Problem of Pain*, C. S. Lewis writes, "You may have noticed that the books you really love are bound together by a secret thread. You know very well what is the common quality that makes you love them, though you cannot put it into words: but most of your friends do not see it at all, and often wonder why, liking this, you should also like that. Again, you have stood before some landscape, which seems to embody what you have been looking for all your life; and then turned to the friend at your side who appears to be seeing what you saw—but at the first words a gulf yawns between you, and you realize that this landscape means something totally different to him, that he is pursuing an alien vision and cares nothing for the ineffable suggestion by which you are transported. Even in your hobbies, has there not always been some secret attraction which the others are curiously ignorant of—something not to be identified with, but always on the verge of breaking through, the smell of cut wood in the workshop or the clap-clap of water against the boat side?

"Are not all lifelong friendships born at the moment when at last you meet another human being who has some inkling (but faint and uncertain in the best) of that something which you were born desiring, and which, beneath the louder passions, night and day, year by year, from childhood to old age, you are looking for, watching for, listening for? You have never *had* it. All the things that have ever deeply possessed your souls have been but hints of it—tantalizing glimpses, promises never quite fulfilled, echoes that died away just as they caught your ear. But if it should really become manifest—if there ever came an echo that did not die away but swelled into the sound itself—you would know it. Beyond all possibility of doubt you would say 'Here at last is the thing I was made for.' We cannot tell each other about it. It is the secret signature of each soul, the incommunicable and unappeasable want, the thing we desired before we met our wives or made our friends or chose our work, and which we shall still desire on our deathbeds, when the mind no longer knows wife or friend or work. While we are, this is. If we lose this, we lose all . . .

"Be sure that the ins and outs of your individuality are no mystery to Him; and one day they will no longer be a mystery to you. The mould in which a key is made would be a strange thing if you had never seen a key: and the key itself a strange thing if you had never seen a lock. Your soul has a curious shape because it is a hollow made to fit a particular swelling in the infinite contours of the divine substance, or a key to unlock one of the doors of the house with many mansions. For it is not humanity in the abstract that is to be saved, but you—you, the individual reader, John Stubbs, or Janet Smith. Blessed and fortunate creature, your eyes shall behold Him and not another's. All that you are, sins apart, is destined, if you will let God have His good way, to utter satisfaction . . . God will look to every soul like its first love because He is its first love. Your place in heaven will seem to be made for you and you alone, because you were made for it—made for it stitch by stitch as a glove is made for a hand."[4]

It would seem that each of us would be in a custom-made *home* in every sense of the word, created by the Master Builder. Heaven will truly be a Master-planned community. Right now preparations are under way for your arrival—and more importantly—your eternal residence. Your needs, desires, and preferences—which even you aren't completely clear about—He knows! Your home will be ready and waiting—like an earthly home decorated to your exact specifications. It will draw you and fulfill you like no other place ever has. Like an earthly home with the smell of good food, the presence of good friends and family and a fire in the fireplace, it will beckon to you. Best of all, Jesus will be there inviting you in.

We tend to focus on the building, wondering what it will look like (and yes, I believe it will be a building of some sort), yet home is more than a building. Home is family, love, contentment, security, the intangibles of life that mean so much to us. In each and every category, your home will be designed for you.

Home Is More Than a Place

I live in Solvang, California, in the United States of America. When I speak of going home, I'm not just talking about the building I live in, but the state, county, and town. When I was recently in Maui, I compared the weather (hot, humid) to the wine country I live in (cooler, less humid). Maui is absolutely gorgeous, and my wife and I practically lived on the beaches, reveling in the beautiful sea and island life, but home for me is wide-open skies at night, filled with thousands of stars and the Milky Way. It is rolling hills with meadows, vineyards, and oak trees. It is cattle and horses grazing on hillsides, hawks soaring overhead, amazing sunrises and sunsets, and the breeze coming up every afternoon. It is country life, the life I love. Geography, weather, and sights and sounds of my town are all part of what I mean when I say "home."

Heaven and earth will somehow be united in a glorious new world that we are forced, for the most part, to imagine, for there is nothing in our world to compare it with. Today the earth and the heavens are part of one world, yet they are separated.

Exploring Home—*Forever!*

We journey with great difficulty from our earthly home to the heavens (stars, moon, planets, and galaxies). We have walked on the moon and sent probes into the reaches of our galaxies, yet only with great difficulty. There are dangers, for our human bodies are not designed to be able to survive in the environment of space. With our greatest technology we cannot truly even think of probing the outer extents of space, for they are too vast for us to reach.

Yet this does not appear to be the case with the new heavens and new earth. With a new heaven and new earth and new glorified bodies like our Lord's, it appears we will be able to travel freely in our new world, for it is ours. It is our inheritance, part of our eternal home. Indeed, it was created for us. We have not even fully explored our world today, though we make a valiant attempt. We probe the depths of the oceans with great difficulty, the vastness of space with Herculean effort, and, with the help of sophisticated technology, attempt to uncover the mysteries beneath the earth's surface; we know that never in our lifetime could we hope to gain all the knowledge that is there or discover all the secrets our world holds.

But that won't be true of the new heaven and new earth. It is quite possible, and even probable, that our human desires to explore and understand, given to us by God, will find their greatest fulfillment in eternity. God has made us to explore and discover with great delight. He is a creative God, who has not only created once but will continually create, for that is His nature. We will constantly be learning, constantly exploring, constantly discovering new truths about the world He will make. And it isn't likely that we'll need spaceships or submarines to do it. Our new glorified bodies will be designed to perfectly fit the new world we will inhabit.

Commentator Albert Barnes writes, "The universe at large will be heaven—the earth and all worlds; and we are left free to suppose that the redeemed will yet occupy any position of the universe, and be permitted to behold the special glories of the divine character that are manifested in each of the worlds that He has made. That there may be some one place in the universe that will be their permanent home, and that will be more properly called heaven, where the glory of their God and Savior will be especially manifested is not improbable; but still there is nothing to prevent the hope and the belief that in the infinite duration that awaits them they will be permitted to visit all the worlds that God has made, and to learn in each, and from each, all that He has especially manifested of His own character and glory there."[5]

We use spaceships and submarines *because we need them, because our bodies are not perfectly fitted to explore our world without them.* But what if that were no longer the case? Jesus, in His glorified body, which is the prototype of ours, was able to ignore the physical obstructions of our planet, like walls, gravity, density, and other things. Though physical Himself, He vanished and appeared, He passed through solid walls, He floated up into heaven defying gravity. Our new bodies will be made perfectly for the new heaven and earth, our heavenly home. We have heard the phrase in history "the golden age of exploration." In reality, that age lies ahead of us, not behind us.

We will have, forever, a brand new world, better by far than our present one, to explore—forever. And we will be fully equipped for the task. As a teenager, when I was sailing to Catalina Island off the coast of California, I would wonder what was beneath the water we were traveling over. In Maui, I was able to snorkel and see just a tiny glimpse of the abundant life and activity that lie beneath the surface of the water. But what if I could explore all those places without a snorkel or oxygen tank? What if I could climb the highest peaks with no danger of freezing or being starved of oxygen? What if I could transport myself to another planet or galaxy because my body had the ability to do that? What if I could fly, overcoming density and gravity? How would that change my ability to fully explore the new home He has made for us?

Will that new world have mountains, valleys, rivers, lakes, trees, flowers, animals, smells, sounds, and places that will stun us with their beauty and wonder? Will our new world have new planets, suns, stars, nebulae, quasars, and things we don't even have in our present solar system? Will there be abundant wildlife that we can mingle among safely, some creatures familiar, others not? Why not? Those things are earthly and heavenly, and God is creating a new heaven and a new earth. That new earth and heaven will be newer, better by far, but still heavenly and earthly, just as our bodies, which will be glorified, will still be bodies.

Our New Home's New Heavenly Capital

"By calling the New Earth, *Earth*, God emphatically tells us it will be earthly, and thus familiar," writes Randy Alcorn. "Otherwise, why call it Earth? When scripture speaks of a 'new song,' do we imagine it's wordless, silent, or without rhythm? Of course not. Why? Because then it wouldn't be a song. If I promised you a new car, would you say, 'If it's new, it probably won't have any engine, transmission, doors, wheels, stereo, or upholstery?' If a new car didn't have these things, it wouldn't be a car. If we buy a new car, we know it will be a better version of what we already have, our old car. Likewise, the New Earth will be a better version of the old Earth.

"The word *new* is an adjective describing a noun. The noun is the main thing. A new car is first and foremost a car. A new body is mainly a body. A New Earth is mainly an earth . . . We're told the 'first earth' will pass away (Rev. 21:1). The word for first is '*prote*,' suggesting a vital connection between the two earths. The first earth serves as the proto-type or pattern for the new earth. There's continuity between old and new. We should expect new trees, new flowers, new rocks, new rivers, new mountains, and new animals. (*New*—not *non*!)"[6]

When we read of the New Jerusalem, the heavenly city, in Revelation 21–22, we read of trees with fruit and avenues. William Hendriksen, a commentator on the Scriptures, suggests, "The term 'tree of life' is collective, just like 'avenue' and 'river.' The idea is not that there is just one single tree. No, there is an entire park: whole rows of trees alongside the river; hence, of the city. Hence, the city is just full of parks, cf. Rev. 2:7. Observe, therefore, this wonderful truth: the city is full of rivers of life. It is also full of parks containing trees of life. These trees, moreover, are full of fruit."[7] If he is right, we can begin to get an idea of what this city will be like as much as we are able. There will be things we recognize.

Furthermore, in the description of the New Jerusalem (Revelation 21– 22), we see the characteristics of a physical place. The city has walls, gates, foundations, streets, a river, trees, leaves, and fruit. We are told that nations will walk by its light, and the kings of earth will bring their splendor into it (Revelation 21:24), indicating governments of people, cultures, and differences in what they bring to offer. Our Lord will be on His throne in this city. The thing that is striking is the color and dazzling architecture of the heavenly city. It seems very possible to me, at least, that this might be the very city that Jesus has gone to prepare for us. (Remember, the new heavens and new earth won't be created until after the great white throne judgment, meaning that this city could be in existence even now). The New Jerusalem comes down out of heaven, thus uniting both worlds (heaven and earth) into one.

Though it is speculative, it is possible that when we die, we go to this city that exists somewhere and is the paradise of God. We might live there until the new heaven and new earth are completed. If so, this would give a very tangible physical place of existence for us when we enter eternity.

The writer of Hebrews tells us, "But you have come to Mount Zion, *to the heavenly Jerusalem, the city of the living God.* You have come to thousands upon thousands of angels in joyful assembly, to the church of the firstborn, whose names are written in heaven" (Hebrews 12:22–23, emphasis added).

Since Jerusalem is the city of the living God, is it, therefore, in existence even now? Have those who have gone before us entered it already? It makes sense that this is where our Lord is, in His city, a physical place of perfect beauty and joy.

The New Jerusalem is laid out like a city, and true to what has been told us, has aspects of a city we are familiar with and aspects that are totally foreign to us. It sounds very much like a city until its dimensions are given. If we take them literally, and since exact measurements are given it appears we are meant to, and we are told that the angel measuring the city was using man's measurements (Revelation 21:17), then the city is 396,000 stories (at 20 feet a story), or an area roughly equivalent to one-half of the United States. It appears that this jewel of a city is perfectly symmetrical, a massive cube, fourteen hundred miles square and fourteen hundred miles high.

That is an astounding city, but shouldn't we expect a city with incredible dimensions? In our present world, fourteen hundred miles high would place the city beyond the atmosphere (ours is only about one hundred miles deep), but at that point heaven and earth will be joined together, so atmosphere will no longer be an issue—and in our glorified bodies, will it matter? In short, the dimensions of the new city leave plenty of room for everyone who is going to heaven, each of us with our own "heavenly acre." Each of God's people from the very beginning of creation will be represented in that city. It's definitely big enough!

We are told that on the gates of this city are written the names of the twelve tribes of Israel, and the city's foundations have written on them the names of the twelve apostles, thus indicating that this place is the permanent home of all believers, those who lived in the Old Testament up to every believer in the church (Revelation 21:12–14).

There are many other vivid descriptions of the city: the walls made of jasper, the foundations of the city made of every kind of precious stones, the twelve gates that are huge pearls, and the streets of gold. I will speak more about this later. Suffice it to say that you can read these descriptions yourself and try to imagine such beauty. Remember, one day you will behold this scene and know it is your home.

Of course we need to mention again that there are those who take these descriptions and measurements as merely symbolic. But then the question has to be asked, symbolic of what? We need to point out, again, that something can be both symbolic and literal. The dimensions given are all multiples of twelve, indicating they have a spiritual meaning. But the original Holy of Holies had spiritual significance, and it was a literal place. The dimensions were both symbolic and literal at the same time.

And though symbolism is used, why are such specific descriptions of stones, colors, and measurements (even going so far as using human measurements) given to simply be symbolic? It appears to me that while some of this is symbolic language, it is attempting to describe a tangible reality.

If I were to try to describe a radically new concept car, one that no one but I had seen, I would have to use terms that were descriptive without being perfectly representative. I would talk about the chassis, and compare it to a car that was as similar as I could think of (maybe a hybrid of a car, a bus, and a motorcycle), using colors of fruit, perhaps, or nature to describe its new color. When you saw the car, you would recognize many of the features I was trying valiantly to describe but also see how different (and better) it was from my weak description. My descriptions were accurate as far as they went; it was a car, similar to my description, but you'd have to see it to get the full impact. This, I believe, is what is happening in Revelation 21. John, the apostle, is gazing on something real, trying to describe it with the best language he has available.

If the idea of a city makes you feel claustrophobic, pastor and author Erwin Lutzer suggests, "You need not fear that you will be lost in the crowd; nor need you fear being stuck on the thousandth floor when all of the activity is in the downstairs lounge. All you will need to do is to decide where you would like to be, and you will be there! Each occupant will receive individualized attention. The Good Shepherd who calls His own sheep by name will have a special place prepared for each of His lambs. There will be a crown awaiting us that no one else can wear, a dwelling place that no one else can enter."[8]

Keep in mind always that this is just the city, the New Jerusalem, not all of heaven. We will not be limited to that home, for all of creation is our inheritance, not just our heavenly acre. Yet it appears that we will all have a home in the capital city.

The Place You Could Only Dream About

God will not just make a building that we can call our own, our own heavenly acre, if you will. He will make everything about heaven home. When we get there we will most likely think, "This is what I've always wanted but could never describe." On initial blush it will probably seem more like a dream than reality. Our first moments in eternity, in paradise, we will finally experience those elusive feelings of finally being home. All our experiences of home that are pleasant and precious to us here on earth were nothing more than cravings for our eternal home. God knew. He made it. It's going to be home—forever.

At the end of C. S. Lewis's book, *The Last Battle*, we read, "Everyone raised his hand to pick the fruit he best liked the look of, and then everyone paused for a second. This fruit was so beautiful that each felt, 'It can't be meant for me . . . surely we're not allowed to pick it.'

"'It's alright,' said Peter. 'I know what we're all thinking. But I'm quite sure we needn't. I've a feeling we've got to the country where everything is allowed.' "[9]

"Heaven means not just a pleasant place but *our* place, not just a good place, but a good place for us. We fit there; we are truly human there," writes Peter Kreeft.[10] Pastor and author John MacArthur adds, "If you're worried about feeling out of place in heaven, don't. Heaven will seem more like home than the dearest spot on earth to you."[11]

Many have feared that heaven as their home will seem strange and foreign. Yet the very opposite is true. What we fear is a heavenly home that isn't really designed so much for human beings as for angels, but that isn't the case. As MacArthur points out, think of those places that mean so much to you here on earth, those places you feel you will miss with such a passion. Then imagine that you suddenly see a scene, a place, that is so wondrous, so amazing, so beautiful, and so enticing that you would gladly leave your memories behind if you could but keep the memory of this scene forever. But this scene isn't just a trick of the imagination; it is your eternal home.

Theologian A. A. Hodge writes, "Heaven, as the eternal home of the divine Man and of all the redeemed members of the human race, must necessarily be thoroughly human in all its structure, conditions, and activities. Its joys and its occupations must all be rational, moral, emotional, voluntary, and active. There must be the exercise of all faculties, the gratification of all tastes, the development of all talent capacities, the realization of all ideals. The reason, the intellectual curiosity, the imagination, the aesthetic instincts, the holy affection, the social affinities, the inexhaustible resources of strength and power native to the human soul, must all find in heaven exercise and satisfaction."[12]

Our Heavenly Home—A Gain, Not a Loss

When we were children, we loved plain sugar cookies, but as we got older, we gladly gave them up for more enticing desserts like hot fudge sundaes, Tiramisu, cherries jubilee, blueberry pie, specialty chocolates, and far, far more. Your heavenly home won't be a loss of anything but a gain that is so great that we will wonder how our old desires held our hearts as much as they did.

However, having demonstrated that heaven is definitely in every way home to us in all the intangible ways that are so important, we must not forget the tangibles of our new home, for it will be very, very tangible. As the loved ones we meet there and are reacquainted with there will be real, tangible people that we can see, touch, talk with, and interact with, so our home will be something we can see, touch, and appreciate in a physical fashion (like the gates and walls of the New Jerusalem). A place that is made for physical humans (remember our resurrected bodies) must itself be very physical and tangible. If it will be made for eternity, it must also be amazing. If the eternal God of creation creates it, it must be beautiful and wondrous enough to enable us to enjoy and be amazed at it *forever!*

I expect to live in a dwelling, a building of some kind. I think it will be decorated and appointed just for me. There might be lots of windows, because I want to see as much of my new world as possible, and lots of doors to open to my family, friends, and new saints I will be meeting for all eternity, each friend as beloved and cherished as the other. My home won't be exactly like anyone else's.

Understanding that we will live forever on a new earth, a physical place, allows us to enjoy this earth we live on now. Too often we feel we shouldn't love this earth, and we base this idea on a misunderstanding of the apostle John's words, "Do not love the world or anything in the world. If anyone loves the world, the love of the Father is not in him" (1 John 2:15). Yet it is not the earthly world that John is speaking of here but the values of the world system that operates under the power of Satan. John goes on to make that clear in the next verses.

"For everything in the world—the cravings of sinful man, the lust of his eyes and the boasting of what he has and does—comes not from the Father but from the world. The world and its desires pass away, but the man who does the will of God lives forever" (1 John 2:16–17). It is clear that the world's values are what we are not to love, for they are satanic values. But God created the earth itself, and it was God Himself who said, "It is *very* good" (Genesis 1:31, emphasis added).

This earth was created for us—and it is not wrong to love it. We must not worship it, for it is but the creation of our God—but we can admit that we do love earth and wait in eager anticipation of our better country, which is the new heaven and earth united forever.

As Randy Alcorn writes, "To say, 'This world is not your home' to a person who's fully alive and alert to the wonders of this world is like throwing a bucket of water on kindling's blaze. We should fan the flames of that blaze to help it spread, not seek to put it out. Otherwise, we malign our God-given instinct to love the earthly home God made for us. And we reduce spirituality into a denial of art, culture, science, sports, education, and all else human. When we do this, we set ourselves up for hypocrisy—for we may pretend to disdain the world while sitting in church, but when we get into the car we turn on our favorite music and head home to BBQ with friends, watch a ball game, play golf, ride bikes, work in the garden, or curl up with a good book. We do these things not because we are sinners, but because we are people."[13]

Though we are free to love this earth, as we have already pointed out in earlier chapters, there is within each of us a longing to find a better home, a better world.

"We are like deep sea divers moving slowly and clumsily in the dim twilight of the depths, and we have our work to do. But this is not our element, and the relief of the diver in coming back to fresh air and sunlight and the sight of familiar faces is but a poor picture of the unspeakable delight with which we shall emerge from our necessary imprisonment into the loveliness and satisfaction of our true home."[14]

Just pause for a moment and realize that right now your eternal home is being created, or is already finished, just waiting your arrival. Everything that in your soul desperately cries out for a home that is perfect will be awaiting you. Not just spiritually, though that is supreme, but also physically. Your home will not just be a "feeling of home" but a tangible place in the new heavens and new earth!

Yours!

Can you even imagine what a place would be like that was made by Jesus just for you? He knows you even better than you know yourself. You have, through your life, "discovered" certain things that you like and things that you love. You weren't aware of them before that moment of discovery, but God was. Knowing what would fulfill you in every possible way, Jesus has built your home.

It is waiting for you—in the better country.

Think of stepping on shore and finding it heaven
Of taking hold of a hand and finding it God's

79

Of breathing a new air and finding it celestial air
Of feeling invigorated and finding it immortality!
Of passing from storm to stress to a perfect calm
Of waking and finding it home![15]

But when we arrive at our new heavenly home, what will the atmosphere be like?

The journey continues.

CHAPTER SIX

The Real Magical Kingdom—
The Atmosphere of Heaven

If we really think that home is elsewhere and that this life is a
"wandering to find home," why should we not look forward to
the arrival?[1]   —C. S. Lewis

When I was a young boy, I visited Disneyland in Anaheim, California, for the first time. I had no idea what to expect. As I walked across the wide, drab parking lot, I couldn't have begun to understand what was behind those walls that shielded the Magic Kingdom from my view. All I had been able to see from any distance was the white-capped Matterhorn Mountain looming over the landscape. (That was many years ago!) As I neared the entrance I could hear music and spied a small train station with a small-scale steam locomotive puffing away above me on tracks.

When I entered the gates of the park, however, everything changed—*suddenly*! Immediately, the gay, happy music grew louder, and, emerging through the entrance tunnel, I saw beautifully manicured trees and gardens with brightly colored flowers blooming dazzlingly. I had entered the quintessential small-town America. The small-scale, gaily trimmed Victorian-style buildings all along Main Street were quaint and designed to evoke every nostalgic and heartwarming feeling inside of me. The visual stimulation was so sudden and powerful that I could not take it all in at once.

But what I remember most clearly was the activity. From the humdrum, boring, mostly empty parking lot, I suddenly encountered a bustling, busy, exciting, and enchanting place. Vintage cars drove slowly down one side of the street, honking their horns, while horse-drawn trolleys filled with happy tourists came down the other. Sounds and sights of people, thousands of them, walking, talking, laughing, eating, running, pointing, and taking pictures created an atmosphere of excitement. Here and there colorful Disney characters like Pluto and Donald Duck were posing for pictures with tourists. An enticing aroma of foods wafted toward me, and each store I passed was filled with colorful souvenirs and candy, the store windows gaily decorated in scenes from my favorite Disney stories.

Everything hit me at once. Every step delivered a new and amazing discovery, a new wonder to explore—Fantasyland, Adventureland, Tomorrowland, Frontierland, New Orleans Square, Tom Sawyer's Island—each filled with colorful scenes, period buildings, exciting rides, and incredible architecture. With each new discovery I was entranced and all the more eager to find the next magical place. I had truly wandered into another world, and my physical and emotional senses were on overload. I soon realized that this exciting and magical place had been here for quite some time, existing even while my boring and often difficult life went on elsewhere. Outside, everything was predictable and ordinary. Here—well, here was something else again.

It appears that entering heaven will be, for us, much like that. Not in any sense like a human Disneyland, but a place and experience so vibrant, alive, colorful, and enchanting that all our human senses threaten to begin blinking "tilt" at our first sighting.

We have been led to believe that entering heaven is much like entering a funeral home or library or great European cathedral, at least in atmosphere. It is pictured often as a place of sanctified and reverent silence, interrupted only by the droning sounds of the singing of ancient hymns. The activity level would approach that of a monastery. Nothing could possibly be further from the truth.

Heaven's Wonders Will Never Cease

The difference between eternal introspective contemplation and sudden overwhelming joy and astonishment is the difference between wrong ideas about the atmosphere of heaven and correct ones. We are told in Scripture that in God's presence is joy (Psalm 16:11; 21:6), and it means exactly that. We've felt joy before, so we will be familiar with the feeling but entirely unfamiliar with the intensity and eternal character and unending causes for that enduring joy. It is a little like someone who has seen only a small pond and is familiar with bodies of water but unprepared for the sight, power, and magnitude of the ocean. It will be a joy that, like every part of the better country, is "better by far."

Our first emotion will most likely be astonishment and wonder at the people we see, sights we behold, and sounds we hear, followed closely by an overwhelming feeling of joy and peace. Like I experienced on my first trip to Disneyland, each new sound and sight of heaven will elicit greater joy and wonder and a corresponding desire for worship. Yet unlike the Disneyland experience, which can be fully enjoyed in a few days and can also include many unpleasant aspects of life on earth (cost, crowding, impatience, fatigue, selfishness), heaven's wonders will be perfect and never cease, nor will we ever be able to fully experience it all.

When we read in the Scriptures of people and angels continually falling down and worshiping in heaven, we inevitably fail to take into account the powerful emotion that is driving this worship. But there is no monotonous, fabricated, or grudging worship in that place. It is the environment of heaven itself—the glory, the joy, the unexpected beauty, and wonder—that create that desire for worship.

Have you ever been someplace so wonderful and unexpectedly beautiful that it took your breath away? The scenes described for us in Revelation 21 and 22 are so dazzlingly beautiful and amazing that spontaneous worship is the natural response, and that is just a response to the place itself, not to the glory and wonder of being in the actual presence of our God. You will worship like you never have before—not because it is required but because you will be feeling and experiencing more powerful things than you ever have before. No longer shall we walk by faith; there faith shall become sight. No longer will we see dimly; there everything will be clear.

It was my experiences at Disneyland at a young age that sent me hurrying to the library to learn about the amazing man who could create such a "magical" place. Heaven, unlike Disneyland, is not manmade, man-inspired, or subject to decay but is eternal; its architect, builder, and creator is God Himself. Its wonders will eternally draw our attention back again and again to its creator and sustainer.

We are drawn in literature and entertainment to magical worlds, such as Narnia, in C. S. Lewis's *Chronicles of Narnia*, or Middle Earth in

J. R. R. Tolkien's *Lord of the Rings* trilogy. Each place exhibits magical qualities that we wish actually occurred on earth but sadly don't. Perhaps that's why we're attracted to these stories. They describe worlds that seem so much better than the world we live in that we grow eager to enter them, even when we know they don't exist.

Yet many people, even some fine Bible commentators, describe heaven in sterile, academic terms. There is little sense of wonder in their descriptions, and yet the biblical descriptions of heaven depict an atmosphere of "magical" proportions in every possible way.

"This deep-seated conviction that heaven may be an eternal bore reflects the sinful thinking of man," writes John MacArthur. "As sinners we are naturally prone to think a little sin is surely more enjoyable than perfect righteousness. It is hard for us to imagine a realm wholly devoid of sin and yet filled with endless pleasures."[2]

It *is* hard for us to imagine a realm wholly devoid of sin and yet filled with endless pleasures because, frankly, it's outside our experience. Ever since Eden, that kind of world has been beyond our reach. The atmosphere we live in on earth—its experiences, its activities, its allures, its attractions, its beauties, and its people—are all sin-infected. We don't know, by experience, how good perfect righteousness can feel. We lack the experience to understand a place that is perfect in every possible way and greater than our deepest longings.

Yet when we study the biblical descriptions of heaven, we are allowed glimpses of the unimaginable. As we explore the atmosphere of heaven we will be looking at our heavenly place—the sounds, sights, and activities of heaven. Yet first we must answer an objection that some have raised: namely, how do we know we'll even be conscious in paradise before the resurrection?

Consciousness in Pre-Heaven

There is abundant scriptural evidence that the moment we die on this earth, we immediately wake to eternal life, enter paradise, and experience consciously all the delights and wonders of heaven in the presence of our Lord. In chapter 4, we discussed pre-heaven, the destination for believers who die before the end of time and the great white throne judgment, and we described what existence will be like for those who live there. It is clear from the Scripture passages that we considered that those who live in pre-heaven will be conscious before the resurrection.

The apostle Paul writes, "Therefore, being always of good courage, and knowing that while we are at home in the body we are absent from the Lord—for we walk by faith, not by sight—we are of good courage, I say, and *prefer rather to be absent from the body and to be at home with the Lord*" (2 Corinthians 5:6–8 NASB, emphasis added). To be absent from the body is to be at home with the Lord. We can hardly call an unconscious state "at home with the Lord."

In Luke 16, in the story of the rich man and Lazarus, we see that the rich man was aware of his surroundings, as was Lazarus. The rich man in his agony was aware of where he was and that his brothers were all going to join him unless they were converted. There was a clear consciousness.

To the church at Philippi, Paul writes, "But I am hard-pressed from both directions, having *the desire to depart and be with Christ, for that is very much better*; yet to remain on in the flesh is more necessary for your sake" (Philippians 1:23–24 NASB, emphasis added). In what way would being unconscious be very much better than being alive and alert on earth where one could still serve one's Lord?

Remember the transfiguration of Christ? Jesus was transfigured before Peter, James, and John, when suddenly Elijah and Moses appeared. We see both of them not only alive but conversing with Jesus, presumably about His coming death and resurrection. This indicates that the people of God are not only conscious after death but also interested and engaged in both earthly and heavenly affairs.

In Revelation 6 we are allowed, with the apostle John, to witness a revealing scene in heaven. John observes the martyrs and hears them crying out. If those who die are unconscious after death until the resurrection, how could these souls cry out to God? Here again we see evidence that when believers are absent from the body they are present with the Lord in a fully conscious and alert state.

Other passages in Isaiah (14:9–11, 15–17) seem to indicate conscious life after death but describe consciousness in hell for unbelievers.

It is important that we address this issue, for a heavenly atmosphere would be a moot point if we were not immediately awake and conscious the instant we die on this earth. There is activity in heaven at this moment; why should we be kept unconscious during this crucial and exciting time on earth when we are, of all beings, most concerned?

Aside from the clear scriptural teaching on this issue, we have ample anecdotal evidence of those believers in Christ who have had near-death experiences and who confirm alertness and awareness immediately following their temporary earthly passing. Again, these experiences can serve to *confirm* what the Bible teaches, not to become authoritative in and of themselves. Scripture is our final authority.

Knowing then that we will be fully aware and conscious when we leave this earth and enter the presence of our Lord in paradise, what then can we expect to experience of the atmosphere of heaven? First, we will deal with place, for the place we are going is paradise, and it has been vividly described for us. Let's take a much deeper look at the New Jerusalem, something we have touched on only briefly before.

The Heavenly City, the New Jerusalem

I believe that this city is the first *place* we will see immediately after we die. Since it is called in Hebrews 12:22 the "city of the living God, the heavenly Jerusalem, and to myriads of angels, to the general assembly and church of the firstborn who are enrolled in heaven" (Hebrews 12:22–23 NASB), we can see that the very description of this city includes all the believers of all ages, with God's holy angels as well. This is the same city that John sees descend out of heaven to come to earth, thus uniting heaven and earth into one new eternal realm in Revelation 21:1, 10. It appears to be the place Jesus told us He had gone to prepare for us (John 14:2–3). So let's see what all the excitement is about, for surely John saw a scene in heaven that filled his eyes and heart with wonder.

The first thing John sees in Revelation 21 is the Holy City, the New Jerusalem "coming down out of heaven from God, prepared as a bride beautifully dressed for her husband" (Revelation 21:2).

The vivid imagery and description of this place begin in verse eleven. We see, first, that the entire city shone like the brightness of a shiny object. This city's chief characteristic visually is that it is brilliantly light and effervescent, like a jasper stone, and clear as crystal. You could fairly describe this as a crystal city, but as we're going to learn, the colors we will see will take our breath away. From a distance, it appears like a polished brilliantly shining jewel, and indeed it should since much of its construction is made of precious jewels.

The city has high walls and ornately gorgeous gates, twelve in all. At each gate is stationed an angel, so before we enter the city, we will definitely have finally laid eyes on an angel.

The city is laid out in either a cube or a pyramid shape, with three gates on each of the four walls. An angel began to measure the city for John according to earthly measurements, which are also angelic measurements. So far it sounds almost like a fairy-tale city, but there's far more.

As we saw in the last chapter, when the city was measured it was determined that it was as long as it was wide, approximately fourteen hundred miles wide, fourteen hundred miles long, and—yes—fourteen hundred miles *high*! The walls are approximately two hundred feet thick. But before you imagine walls that shield what is inside from your eyes, look again carefully. Though thick, these walls are made of jasper, a precious stone that can appear in a variety of different colors and patterns. It is an opaque stone normally, yet here the jasper is clear like crystal. What exact color is represented here we can't determine, but what is clear is that the walls appear to reflect and transmit light, not block it. "The constant mention of transparency indicates that the city is designed to transmit the glory of God in the form of light without hindrance."[3]

The city overall has a golden appearance, but not the type of gold we see on earth. In the New Jerusalem the gold is more translucent with a golden hue (Revelation 21:18). The huge brilliant foundation stones are each precious jewels. The foundation was a huge stone that often sat both under the ground and slightly above the ground to serve as the base upon which the rest of the wall sat. The foundation stones and their approximate color (though these change, so we can't be precise) are as follows:

- jasper—of a crystal-clear variety, unlike earthly versions, which are opaque
- sapphire—blue
- chalcedony—sky blue, with stripes of color throughout it
- emerald—brilliant bright green

- sardonyx—red and white
- sardius—(in some versions rendered "carnelian") reddish and honey color
- chrysolyte—transparent golden (Pliny's description of the ancient stone—possibly different from today)
- beryl—sea green
- topaz—yellow/green and transparent
- chrysoprase—shade of green
- jacinth—violet
- amethyst—purple

Many of these stones appeared in the high priest's breast piece in Exodus 28:15–21.

Imagine each of these foundation stones brilliantly illuminating color up through the crystal jasper walls and reflecting vivid hues and dazzlingly bright colors everywhere as the glory of the city shines upon you. Each gate is "pearlescent" in the sense that each one is made of one huge pearl. Some commentators have urged us to see this as simply figurative language, since they point out it would take an oyster of enormous size to create such a pearl. We need to remember, however, that God does not need an oyster to make a pearl, since He created everything out of nothing, simply speaking creation into existence (Hebrews 11:3). This is not a super *human* city; it is the *heavenly* city, the city of the living God, and we should expect that its description and dimensions *would* in some ways defy earthly explanation.

John describes the streets of the city as a pure, though translucent, gold. There is no temple in this city, for our God, the Lamb, is its temple. There is no need for the sun or the moon to illuminate this city forever, for God's glory, the glory of the Lamb, is its light. The Bible does not say, by the way, that there will be no sun or moon, only that they are not necessary for their previous functions. The gates will never be shut, and they will be in continual usage as the nations walk in and out and the "kings of the earth" bring their splendor into it.

This city will be busy, bustling, and glorious in every way, defying comparison to any earthly city we have known in history or see today. It will be the capital city of the people of God for all eternity, not encasing the believers forever in its beautiful walls but providing a residence for them as they surely travel to other parts of God's vast creation. That people will live in or travel to other places than this city in eternity is clear by virtue of the fact that they bring their glory into the city from outside.

"The New Jerusalem will have the distinction of being the residence of the saints, but it is implied that they will be able to travel elsewhere on the new earth and possibly also in the New Heaven."[4]

Within this city, we see in Revelation 22, is a river of life that flows from the throne of our God down the middle of a great street in the city (not the only street, but the "great" one, apparently the main thoroughfare). There are trees on both sides of this river, creating a beautiful park-like atmosphere within the city and its main street.

"The tree of life spreads all along the great street of the city (v. 2) . . . In Ezekiel's vision these are multiple trees on each side of the river that bear fruit monthly, whose leaves are for the healing (Ezekiel 47:12). Therefore, the tree (xylon) John speaks of may be a collective word for Ezekiel's trees."[5]

This describes a park in the heavenly city, with fruit trees that are for the "healing of the nations." This does not mean we still need to be healed, for the word *healing* is *therapeian,* from which the English word *therapy* is derived. It indicates that the fruit is health giving, or for the promotion of the enjoyment of life in this new world, not for healing ills which no longer exist.

This will be an integral part of the atmosphere of heaven during the pre-heaven period as well as for all eternity, since I believe this city exists even now and will exist forever in eternity. This will be your city, and we are seeing only a fraction of its wonders and even those through the filter of imperfect human descriptions. But of what we can see, I hope you will agree that the atmosphere of heaven is not going to be dull, boring, or anticlimactic.

But we know that this place is a city for the people of God, so now let's look at who lives there.

The Citizens of Heaven

In considering the atmosphere of heaven, it is good to begin with those for whom heaven, or paradise, was made. It was made for people, for their eternal enjoyment and fulfillment. It was made for us to glorify and glory in the person and presence of our God, our Lord Jesus Christ. Therefore we should expect—first and foremost—to see many, many people. In fact, we should be expecting to see many more showing up after we arrive, joining the millions who are already there.

Now I know that some of us are reserved, retiring, and shy by nature. The idea of a big crowd is intimidating or even frightening. To worry that heaven won't be fun or enjoyable for us because of all the people who are there presupposes that we will feel then exactly the same way we feel today.

Heaven will be a city of new people—regenerated, renewed, and perfected. You can never look forward to heaven's atmosphere unless you realize this. The very things that make us shy away from people, the hurtful things they can say, the regretful way they can act, the unfortunate way they often treat us, will no longer even be possible. Our own weaknesses, which sabotage our deeper relationships here on earth, will also be gone forever from us. Heaven is not merely a perfection of place; it is a perfection of people.

"The highest bliss in heaven (save God) shall surely be hearts opened to each other in pure transparency."[6]

Imagine upon arriving in heaven that you discovered, to your delight, that the first person you met loved you so dearly and deeply that it fairly took your breath away and that this expression of love neither embarrassed you nor made you feel strange. You were able to receive this person's love as easily as he or she was able to give it. Then imagine the next person you met loved you with an equivalent, but unique, perfect love. That's the citizenry of heaven. We will speak more about this in a future chapter, but suffice it to say that no citizens will want to hide in a corner or isolate themselves in the presence of these people made new by Jesus. We will truly and genuinely find those relationships our souls have always longed for *among every single citizen of heaven.*

People you have never met will have a capacity for loving and accepting you that defies human experience on earth. In a strange way, there is truly no one on earth that can love you as much as complete strangers in heaven will love you. For here, all our love is sin-infected and sin-affected. The best of our loves has to struggle with resentment, envy, jealousy, pride, anger, and other sinful ingredients. In heaven, each person will be a new "best friend."

We long for the day when we can no longer hurt with our words. It will be perfect bliss to be able to speak everything that is on our minds freely, not needing to worry about whether we are sinning with what we say or think. So many people have been hurt by the things I have said or done, often without any malice on my part. I didn't know the implications of what I was saying; I didn't know how someone would take what I said. I wonder if we've ever had a completely honest conversation on this earth with anyone. We always hold back with others, wondering if they are getting tired of the conversation, wondering what they are thinking of what we are saying, wondering how they are now judging us.

What will heaven be like when we can converse with anyone anywhere on any subject with complete freedom and joy? We won't feel something and be hesitant to say it. We won't want to shout with joy and keep it in. We won't want to share our deepest inner feelings and wonder if anyone really wants to hear them.

But mostly I yearn for the day when I won't sin with my words or with my mind. We often think of heaven in strictly a geographical sense. But heaven, to me, will be as much about having freedom of thought and expression untainted by sin. I won't have to pretend to be something I'm not, to say things that aren't true to make the right impression, to exaggerate in order to try and get people to do something. For the first time in my life, my thoughts will be clear, lucid, unimpeded by sin, deep, unbroken, and completely pure. I will truly care about God's glory, not my own. I will truly love people more than myself. For these are kingdom traits that we are to cultivate now that will one day be the air that we breathe. We won't have to try to do these things; they will be more natural than breathing is here.

This is no ordinary place we are going, and so ordinary people will not populate it. No two people in heaven will be alike. You will not be arriving in a place where everyone is an automaton. All those present will have their own personalities, their own uniquenesses, created in them by God for His glory in eternity. Each person will stimulate and attract us. We won't be dodging people in heaven, finding our quiet corner to sit and escape annoying people.

Some will surely wonder how we will understand people whose language we don't speak, since we know that there will be people from every nation, tribe, and tongue represented in heaven. The Tower of Babel (Genesis 11:1) was where God confused the languages of the people on earth, and that situation will be changed *because the reason* for His confusing the languages will be eliminated. Our ambition as a people will be holy and glorifying to God.

In heaven the world will again have one language and a common speech. John heard the voices of *"every created thing which is in heaven and on earth"* in Revelation 5:13 speaking *with one voice*, which would be impossible unless we have been somehow changed. We will all understand one another. What language will we speak? We don't know, nor do we need to. We will be able to understand one another, so perhaps it will be an entirely new language that we will all know intuitively, or we will simply be able to understand all languages.

I am convinced that the heavenly world God will make for us is only a small part of the wonderful discoveries we will make throughout eternity. What will it be like to discover that we can develop the deepest of friendships and relationships with each and every person in the kingdom of heaven? We will not just be busy with the discovery of the new world God has made for us but of the new people He has made us to be. Each person adds to who we are, as we add to who every other person is, and together we are His body.

This is part of the atmosphere of heaven we can expect to enter. But as we consider the atmosphere of heaven, we must consider an element that so drastically affects our atmosphere on earth: time.

Heavenly Time

One of the greatest stresses in our lives is time—or the lack of it. How much pressure is exerted on us because we have such a limited amount of time? Our entire lives become stressed because we are trying so desperately to accomplish so much under the constant stress of time.

What would our pursuits be like if that pressure were suddenly and permanently removed? "Hurry up" will be a meaningless phrase in heaven and, thus, never uttered. Hallelujah!

We can expect that the passing of time will be drastically different from on earth. Time won't necessarily cease to be, but it will cease to be significant. As Bilbo Baggins in *The Hobbit* observes about the amazing elven city Rivendell, which symbolizes that final eternal state of mankind, "Time doesn't seem to pass here: it just is. A remarkable place altogether."[7] I'm not sure we can quite imagine a place, or even an atmosphere, where time is not chasing us down or breathing down our neck, reminding us of aging bodies, forgotten responsibilities, impending deadlines, or "to do" lists.

For the first time in our lives, we can truly and finally . . . rest. Observing the boundaries of time drives us to worry and fret that we won't finish what we need or want to do or that we won't have the time to do well what we want to do. We often think of heaven as a place without time, when, in reality, it is finally the place where we have all time. As much as we need, to do whatever we want to do, the right way, without deadlines and pressure.

As a husband, father, pastor, and author, that alone would seal the deal for me. I seem to have so little time, and a common affliction of the aging is upon me—time is gaining speed. How many of our physical ailments are caused by stress brought on by deadlines and time issues? I do not desire the rest of inactivity; I deeply desire *the rest of time* to accomplish, and accomplish well, what my gifts and talents will allow me for my Lord.

Our earthly experiences have taught us to say, "All good things must come to an end." Yet when we enter paradise, all good things will just be beginning. We often wish we could rewind our lives to certain experiences and moments and just live in those moments forever because they were so perfect and precious to us and ended way too soon. But in the atmosphere of heaven, those moments will surround us on every side, our constant companions, each one adding to others we have experienced, going on forever.

When we have just finished a delicious meal, we are no longer hungry. When we have taken a long refreshing drink, we are no longer thirsty. There is a feeling, only momentary of course, of complete satisfaction. We have not just sated our hunger or our thirst; we have been pleasantly satisfied. The cravings and longings have been subdued for the moment—but on earth it is always just for the moment. Like ice in the blazing desert sun or a small fire in the freezing arctic, these satisfactions are foreign to the natural condition on earth and have no staying power. A delicious, delightful meal with friends can be followed up with a flat tire on the way home. Perfect moments can't last.

But what if that delicious feeling of fulfillment never left? What if that temporary euphoria we feel after a delicious long afternoon nap or the completion of a work of art we are happy with or the enjoyment of cuddling a newborn puppy never ended? Imagine that the wonderful feeling didn't go away; in fact, the feeling grew stronger and stronger. There is no emotional fatigue that will finally settle in and snatch that feeling away, no other shoe that will finally drop, no future event that can ever affect it negatively. You soon realize that this feeling, this joy, this fulfillment, this awesome sense of wonder and excitement is yours forever. In this place God has made for you to live, the perfect atmosphere outside only compliments the perfect new settings of your heart. We haven't been re-programmed like robots; we've finally returned to the original purpose of our design. Heaven. Forever.

"This present life is interpenetrated by the Real World far more than we know. For most of us it is only very occasionally that we get our flashes of conviction, and it is of immeasurable comfort to know, on authority of that Personal Visit, that our feeble intuition was right and that this short earthly life, important and significant though it may be in its setting, is no more than a Prelude to a share in the timeless life of God."[8]

Time will finally be on our side.

Singing in Heaven

We must not forget that the atmosphere of heaven will be an auditory experience as well as a visual one. You can't read the Revelation and not "hear" the sounds of heaven. John often heard angels or voices speaking to him. (Revelation 1:10; 4:1; and 5:11 are a few examples.) In fact, at one time John heard "every created thing which is in heaven and on the earth and under the earth and on the sea, and all things in them, . . . saying, 'To Him who sits on the throne, and to the Lamb, be blessing and honor and glory and dominion forever and ever.' And the four living creatures kept saying, 'Amen.' And the elders fell down and worshiped" (Revelation 5:13–14 NASB).

In Revelation 14:2 John heard "a voice from heaven, like the sound of many waters and like the sound of loud thunder, and the voice which I heard was like the sound of harpists playing on their harps" (Revelation 14:2 NASB). Please note that John says these sounds were "like" the sound of many waters and "like" the sound of loud thunder and "like" the sound of many harpists. He's using the only words he can to convey a sound that is not altogether familiar. There will be sounds we will hear only in heaven; they simply have no equivalent on earth.

Then, John ends the book with "I, John, am the one *who heard* and saw these things" (Revelation 22:8 NASB, emphasis added). He heard music and singing and celebrations. Sound is a vital part of the atmosphere anywhere, so we should expect that the sounds of heaven will be incredible. We are told by our Lord in Luke 15:7, 10 that "there will be more rejoicing in heaven over one sinner who repents than over ninety-nine righteous persons who do not need to repent . . . There is rejoicing in the presence of the angels of God over one sinner who repents."

These celebrations are taking place in heaven *continually*; they must be. Over thirty-five years ago, some saints must have heard a wonderful celebration begin because one Danny Schaeffer was born again and granted heavenly citizenship. Over and over there will be celebrations because someone who was lost has been rescued, saved from eternal punishment. Who will be doing this celebrating? The angels might be celebrating, but the text actually states that the celebrating is done *in their presence*, not by them, although I certainly think they are celebrating as well. The people of God will be celebrating His victories on earth all during our time in pre-heaven (paradise). That includes you and me.

How different is what heaven rejoices over than what we rejoice over. In our world, we applaud great talent, great ability, great performances, and great accomplishments—yet heaven does not. One sinner, in the quietness of her heart, repents of her attitude toward God, toward Jesus, and her own sin, and our world is largely unaware and unimpressed. But in heaven celebrations begin. One can't help in this day wondering if the church is as captivated by the drama of redemption as she is with "successful" ministries, politics, and famous Christian personalities.

And will we not hear the rushing of water flowing from the throne of God (Revelation 22:1) through the city streets of New Jerusalem? The sounds of people talking, shouting, rejoicing, laughing, eating, and singing will certainly fill our ears; these will be the sounds of supernatural human interaction with man and with God. Will there possibly be the sounds of animals in heaven? I think it is highly likely (see appendix).

And will we suddenly forget all our favorite songs of praise and worship? I hardly think so; in fact, I believe we will finally be able to sing them perfectly and with an absolutely pure heart of worship. The continual sounds of both spontaneous and planned songs of worship will likely fill our senses.

Crying in Heaven

I know that we are told that there will be no more crying and no more tears in heaven. "He will wipe away every tear from their eyes; and there will no longer be any death; there will no longer be any mourning, or crying, or pain; the first things have passed away"(Revelation 21:4 NASB). But if you read closely, you will see that the crying or tears spoken of here are tears of sadness, pain, and loss. However, we also cry when we are happy or deeply moved.

When we are so happy that tears come, we don't sob or wail, we laugh and rejoice. As a result, I believe it is entirely possible that there will be many tears of joy in heaven. But there will be no other kind in that final place. What could be a more pleasing gift of praise to God? If I am wrong about the tears (and that is, of course, possible), I am certain that in some other way we will be able to display the greater emotions we will feel than words could possibly express, even perfect words spoken from hearts and lips finally made perfect.

Serving in Heaven

Perhaps David Head said it best when he wrote, "Lord, I've been active all my life. This idea of eternal rest frightens me. The Beatific something-or-other they talk about in sermons doesn't mean a thing to me. I shall be thoroughly miserable if all I have to do is gaze and gaze. Isn't there anything to do in heaven?"[9] The answer to that question is a resounding yes! Our life won't be spent in detached viewing but in active doing. Heaven will be filled with people and angels serving God in different ways.

"No longer will there be any curse. The throne of God and of the Lamb will be in the city, *and His servants will serve Him*" (Revelation 22:3–4, emphasis added).

We are told in Scripture that our faithfulness here will result in greater authority and responsibility in eternity (Matthew 24:45–51; Luke 12:41–48; 1 Corinthians 3:8, 14; 6:2–3; Colossians 3:24; 2 Timothy 2:12; 2 John 1:8; Revelation 5:10; 11:18; 20:6; 22:5, 12). What we do here has a direct correspondence to our service in heaven. We will all have a service to render to Christ in heaven, a job, a calling, but it won't be one we regret or dislike. It will be a service that defines and fulfills us as nothing we have ever done on this earth could. We will *finally* be doing the thing God designed us to do, and every fiber of our being will be excited and eager to do this service for Christ.

We will rule and reign with our Lord, over others, as others rule and reign over us. The least in heaven will still be great, because everyone will be great there. Yet some will have deserved a greater reward for their service, a greater honor. No one will begrudge them their place, for each person will be ruling us as Christ would, as we will be ruling others as Christ would. Since none of us can imagine a perfect government, we don't look forward to one, but one is coming that we will serve and rejoice in.

When I was younger I wanted desperately to be an important person in heaven. As I have gotten older I confess that I will be happy to have the least honor and lowest position, and that is not false modesty. To live and serve in the eternal kingdom that is coming, over which Christ shall reign, to live in the eternal city, to explore the creation of God forever is enough for me and far more than I deserve. All I am and all I can do is a gift from God. But to know that I will have a particular function, one designed for me before the creation of the old world, one entrusted to me and me alone, is amazing to me.

Now some may hear that and get discouraged, thinking, "I need a rest from work and serving others, not a whole eternity of it!" But think of that activity you most loved doing on earth and the joy it brought you. Maybe it was building something or performing in some way or helping someone do something or being involved with others in a worthwhile project. When you were busily involved in it, you weren't frustrated; you were fulfilled, intent on one purpose, excited, and eager to continue. Such will be the nature of our service to God. Neither fatigue nor boredom will be a problem. After all, you will be serving Jesus directly, able to see His joy and pleasure at all times in what you do for Him.

It appears that we were designed by God to serve Him in a unique way, a way that only we can serve Him, by virtue of our unique creation and gifting. It will, of course, be similar to others' work, but not quite the same. Many artists can paint the same scene but will do so with different hues, colors, and styles. Each brings out something the others' didn't, each complimenting the others' work.

"Once heaven is attained . . . the will does not rest in boredom. Nor does it work in frustration. It rejoices in play . . . It doesn't matter how long it takes because it has no goal beyond its own activity. It is not like climbing a mountain; it is like just walking or exploring, or breathing, singing, better yet, it is living—you are quite happy never to come to the end."[10]

"The universe, so vast and wonderful, seems to have been made to be suited to the eternal contemplation of created minds, and in this universe there is an adaptation for the employment of mind forever and ever."[11]

"We will be busy in the most wondrous possible way," wrote author and pastor Ray Stedman. "There will be new planets to develop, new principles to discover, new joys to experience. Every moment of eternity will be an adventure of discovery."[12]

We will probably be praying in heaven, though in a much newer and intimate way with our Lord. Are the prayers of the saints in Revelation 5:8 limited only to those who are alive on earth? We don't know. But certainly the children of God in paradise have intimate access to our Lord and beseech Him.

A popular question is whether we can expect to see animals in heaven. We certainly see them represented in the book of Revelation (19:11–14, for example). Animals would definitely bring a wonderful atmosphere to not only the New Jerusalem but also eternity on the new earth and new heavens as well. This is a lengthy subject, and I urge you to see the appendix at the end of the book for further information. Essentially, I believe we will see animals of all kinds in heaven and certainly in the new earth and new heavens. But, like the animals described in the millennium, when the wolf grazes with the sheep and the lion lies down with the lamb, the curse of sin will be removed from them as well, ushering in a new relationship between the animal and human kingdoms.

Conversations in Heaven

What will be the topics of discussion in eternity, either in pre-heaven or the new heavens and new earth? If you can't think of anything you might speak to anyone about, consider a few of these.

Topics of Discussion with Other Children of God in Heaven

- Our salvation—how did we come to know our Savior?
- How God worked in hidden ways to help us and deliver us in so many instances.
- What eternal life really means and implies. (Do we really think we can comprehend it all now?)
- Whose life did we affect on earth for Christ without knowing it?
- The clearing up of all earthly mysteries (Why did this happen? Why was that allowed?) without the anger or resentment we carry with us now.
- The explanation of Scriptures that are still confusing. (Remember Jesus explaining His truth to the disciples on the road to Emmaus in Luke 24:13–27?)
- Learning the history and experiences of Old and New Testament Bible heroes of the faith. (What was parting the Red Sea like? What was it like in the lions' den, Daniel?)
- Learning about some of Christ's earthly miracles in greater detail from the apostles.
- Thanking those whose faithfulness to Christ helped lead us to Jesus and thus to heaven itself—and sharing with them how my fruit is theirs as well.
- Meeting those who might have prayed for me in my life without my knowing it and what they helped to accomplish in my life by their prayers alone.
- Speaking with Adam and Eve: What was Eden really like?

Topics of Discussion with Our Lord

- For what was I really made?
- In what way can I serve You and glorify You perfectly, forever?
- How will some of my still-unanswered prayers end?
- Why me? Of all those you could have chosen for salvation, why me?
- Help me to better understand Your glorious tri-unity.
- How did you protect me on earth in ways I never imagined?
- How did You use me in ways I didn't know?
- What happened to You after You were crucified? Where did You go? What did You do?
- Who and what are You going to make me become and do forever?
- What will happen to my children, and to theirs?
- How were angels and demons active in my life in ways I never knew?
- How did You make our world?
- What will the new heavens and new earth be like?
- What is my new name, and what does it mean (Revelation 2:17)?

Topics of Discussion with Angels

- When were you created?
- How did you help us?
- What was Satan's rebellion like?
- What are your battles like? How do you fight?
- What are your powers and abilities, and how do they differ from ours?
- How did you work in the past on earth?
- What was Eden like?
- Did I ever entertain you (Hebrews 13:2)?

These are only a small sampling of the questions and discussions we could have with each other and angels and even our Lord. In fact, someone could rightly ask: How can we know we will be able to ask, or will even be interested in asking, these questions? We don't, but I believe we can surmise from the biblical evidence. We certainly will not be mute or isolated from each other in heaven—just the opposite. We will be social in ways we never were before.

Will I actually even want to ask questions when I get to heaven? I don't know. Will these issues be on our minds anymore? Again, I don't know, but if they are, questions won't be discouraged. It certainly appears from Revelation 6:10 where the martyrs of the faith are asking our Lord a significant question that there are not only questions left to be asked but permission to ask them. If everyone had the same question, we can assume discussions have taken place about this issue among the saints of God. We will still have a few questions along the way regarding the future, but how about our past?

Will we converse with the angels? Why not? Many times in Scripture angels spoke with men and women. Will Jesus be too busy to speak with us? No, that's the whole point of Immanuel, God with us. We will be near Him and see Him as He is, and He will live among us in an intimacy we can't even imagine. We will speak more of that in another chapter, for surely that is the gravy and dessert of heaven for the true follower of Christ: being with Him, seeing Him, speaking with Him—forever.

Eating in Heaven

We are told that we will all be present at the marriage supper of the Lamb, that great celebration of the final fulfillment of the kingdom of God (Revelation 19:9). Again, Jesus reminded us that one day, in the kingdom, we will again eat and drink. " 'For I say to you, I shall never again eat it until it is fulfilled in the kingdom of God.' And when He had taken a cup and given thanks, He said, 'Take this and share it among yourselves; for I say to you, I will not drink of the fruit of the vine from now on until the kingdom of God comes' " (Luke 22:16–18 NASB).

One day there will be a celebration of our Lord's new kingdom, and we will eat and drink again with our new glorified bodies. Eating and drinking will again be something we do, though not for survival. Jesus ate and drank after His resurrection (Luke 24:40–43). He did it then to prove the reality of His physical body and that He was not just a spirit but was real flesh and bone. Our bodies, as His, will not only be able to eat and drink but will finally find their true meaning and purpose. The fruit of the trees of life will be one of our delightful enjoyments (Revelation 22:2).

There are many things that will probably affect the atmosphere of heaven, but hopefully the point has been made that the atmosphere of heaven promises to be anything but boring or dull.

It is into this eternally new, eternally fresh, eternally stimulating, eternally wondrous atmosphere that our earthly death will usher us. It is ironic that we, of all people, would fear leaving this life and this world to enter the next. Our lives in heaven would make an enchanting fairytale if it weren't true—but as it is true, it is beyond all fairytales, beyond all hopes and wishes and dreams.

The breezes of heaven are rustling the leaves of our world, reminding us of its presence and its promise. The last, ultimate, true "magical kingdom" is preparing for your arrival.

Sixteenth-century reformer Martin Luther commented, "I would not give one moment of heaven for all the joys and riches of the world, even if it lasted for thousands and thousands of years."[13] But while the atmosphere of heaven will be wondrous, it is not the main attraction. The real question is this: What will it be like to finally be in His presence—forever?

The journey continues.

PART THREE
Heavenly Life

The life we were always meant to live

CHAPTER SEVEN

In His Presence

I will see God; I myself will see him with my own eyes—I,
and not another. How my heart yearns within me!

(Job 19:26–27).

One day my God will look me in the eyes, and I will look Him in the eyes. Even as I write these words, that thought takes my breath away. It sounds almost sacrilegious or heretical to say that—especially since the Bible makes it clear that "God is spirit" (John 4:24). Yet that same eternal, omnipotent, omniscient, omnipresent God who is spirit became Immanuel, God with us (Matthew 1:23). Revelation 22:4 says that "they will see His face, and His name will be on their foreheads."

Jesus.

To see God today, unveiled, is impossible. He is invisible (Colossians 1:15; 1 Timothy 1:17) and dwells in unapproachable light (Psalm 104:2; 1 Timothy 6:16), and anyone who looked upon Him would die (Exodus 33:20). Yet the promise of God is that in heaven we will finally see Him. Really see Him.

One day we will be in the physical intimate presence of our Creator, our Lord, and our Savior. His relationship with us will be more personal and intimate than any human relationship we have ever experienced on earth.

When our God took on human form and nature, it made it possible for us to physically see Him and perceive Him in a brand new way. Paul reminds us that "in Christ all the fullness of the Deity lives in bodily form" (Colossians 1:19–20; 2:9). When Paul made this statement under the inspiration of the Holy Spirit, Jesus was resurrected and ascended to heaven. Paul didn't say all the fullness of deity *lived* in bodily form, but lives—present tense. Though our omnipresent Lord is not limited to His bodily form, He eternally inhabits it with perfect divine awareness and attentiveness forever in His glorified humanity. In other words, being able to see Him in one place physically in heaven will not prevent Him from being everywhere present at the same time. His humanity does not limit His deity.

Being able to finally see our God is the fulfillment of many prophecies. It is also a reminder that only after God has perfected us through His grace will we be able to see Him and live.

" 'But,' he said, 'you cannot see my face, for no one may see me and live . . . Then I will remove my hand and you will see my back; but my face must not be seen.' " So spoke the Lord to Moses in the book of Exodus (33:20, 23).

"I know that my Redeemer lives, and that in the end he will stand upon the earth. And after my skin has been destroyed, yet in my flesh I will see God; I myself will see him with my own eyes—I, and not another. How my heart yearns within me!" (Job 19:25–27). Job knew that one day he would see his God, his Savior.

"I will put my dwelling place among you, and I will not abhor you. I will walk among you and be your God, and you will be my people" (Leviticus 26:11–12).

"Father, I want those you have given me to be with me where I am, and to see my glory, the glory you have given me because you loved me before the creation of the world" (John 17:24).

"I will live with them and walk among them, and I will be their God, and they will be my people" (2 Corinthians 6:16).

"God, the blessed and only Ruler, the King of kings and Lord of lords, who alone is immortal and who lives in unapproachable light, whom no one has seen or can see. To Him be honor and might forever" (1 Timothy 6:15–16).

"We shall be like him, for we shall see him as he is" (1 John 3:2).

One day I will not only be able to look into the eyes of my God but will be able to physically embrace the one who died for me and who loved me in spite of my sins. Of all the thoughts we can reflect upon about heaven, this one is the greatest. When I hug my Master I will be hugging flesh and bone—yet eternal deity as well. Certainly we will be able to express at least as much human affection toward our Lord in heaven as His earthly disciples did while He was here on earth. The truth is that we will be able to express much, much more—forever. It is the mystery of the incarnation, when God became a man (Philippians 2:5–8), that forever we can perceive Him better, nearer.

He who is omnipresent does not cease to be so by inhabiting human form. He who walked the dusty streets of Palestine, who touched the blind and healed the sick at the same time, was also filling all things (Ephesians 1:23) and was intimately present in galaxies thousands of light years away.

I will finally come home to live with my God, my Father, my Lord—in His presence—forever. It is the single most attractive and compelling part of heaven. And, upon reflection, it is perhaps the most misunderstood.

A Private Audience with Jesus

Today, only in my prayers can I have a private audience with my Lord and my God. Yet one day that will change. As Jesus scheduled a private audience with Peter after His resurrection, so too will we receive one. I believe that when we enter eternal life the angels will take us to our Lord for a private audience, and over eternity, we will experience unlimited private audiences with our Lord. Finally I won't have to wonder what He is thinking or wanting from me. I will know, for He will tell me.

Personally. Privately. Intimately.

I will finally receive the assurance of things hoped for, the reality of things unseen. I will see Him as He is. And He will speak to me, and for the first time I will understand perfectly, comprehend perfectly all He wants me to know. With my human limitations and the curse of sin lifted, He will be able to reveal Himself to me, and I will be able to truly understand Him.

Many years ago, as a young Christian, I could have imagined shame or fear at this meeting with my Lord. I did not understand what Jesus had truly accomplished for me on the cross. His death accomplished peace between God and me, removing the barrier of sin that had been the cause of the hostility, removing that barrier forever by His perfect sacrificial death (Romans 5:1, 8–11; 8:1; Ephesians 2:13–22; 1 Peter 3:18). I have access today to His presence and complete and total acceptance before Him because of what Jesus did, not because of my own goodness (Ephesians

2:8–9, 18; 3:11–12; Titus 3:4–5). Accepting His work on my behalf by faith, I trust in His righteousness, not mine (Romans 3:22; 10:3–4; 2 Corinthians 5:21).

Though today I still wear the baggage of my sinful nature, then I will be able to perfectly perceive the righteousness of Christ given to me as a part of my eternal inheritance.

The parable of the prodigal son (Luke 15:11–32) gives us a glimpse of the heart of our God toward us as we observe the reaction of the prodigal's father—who rejoiced at the return of his son with love, acceptance, and celebration. The mood will not be subdued when the former prodigal (me) finally comes home for good. Unless we understand the attitude of our God toward us today, we can never begin to realize how He will receive us for all eternity.

What Will It Be Like?

Words will never be sufficient to describe this intimacy of relationship with our God—for there is nothing on earth, or in all of human history, to compare. Even Eden is not a perfect example, since Adam and Eve were not yet tested and their access to God's presence was still conditioned. Our relationship with Him will be permanent, eternal, and unchangeable.

What will it be like to have instant and continual access to our Lord for all eternity? We must not conclude that since our Lord will be in a glorified human body for all eternity that He will, therefore, be unable to meet with us when we seek His face because He is "busy with someone or something else.", We will not need to schedule appointments for all eternity in hopes of speaking with our God. Today, many millions of His followers have His complete and undivided attention simultaneously through prayer. Do we think that heaven will be a step back in our intimacy with God?

Heaven is designed to bring God and man into perfectly intimate fellowship forever. It is *better by far* than our present situation! In a way we don't yet fully understand, we will be constantly in the presence of our Lord and God in the most real and tangible way possible.

We are told in Revelation 21:22 that there will be no temple in heaven because He will be our temple. We will no longer need to seek Him out in the holy place—His presence will fill every place, wherever we go, to the farthest reaches of the new heavens and new earth. How can He be both local and tangible and yet omnipresent for all eternity? We cannot explain it any more than we can explain that our Lord is both fully man and fully God. Because we cannot imagine such a thing does not mean it isn't true, however.

Could the Old Testament saints have foreseen the incarnation—when the eternal God became a man? They were completely aware of God's omnipresence (Psalm 139) and the seeming impossibility of God, the omnipresent one, becoming a physical being in a particular localized place. Yet that is what happened. It is a trustworthy statement that if it cannot be imagined, God can do it (Matthew 19:25–26).

Present in His Person

Today, in our world, our Lord is present not only in a place in heaven but also everywhere at once in the person of the Holy Spirit, living in and with us (Psalm 139:7–10; John 14:16–17; 1 Corinthians 3:16). Yet today, in our world, though the Spirit of God is everywhere, we do not often sense, and never see, Him. Yet in heaven we will be changed. Not only will our God be revealed far more clearly to us, but also our ability to comprehend Him will be dramatically and eternally changed.

In the Old Testament, the prophet Elisha asks God to show others all the armies of angels that are hidden from human eyes and senses (2 Kings 6:15–17). The angels were there, but it was only through a special dispensation that merely human eyes could see them. In eternity the veil that has long covered our eyes will be removed, and faith shall be sight. We will not travel "to where God is." In eternity that thought will simply not correspond to the new reality.

We will constantly be in our Lord's presence, not just in some intangible or faith sense but in His presence in an immediate, personal, and continual way. This truth not only boggles our mind, it invigorates our hope. Intimate face-to-face communication with our God will be the new way of life in the new heavens and new earth.

No longer will our God be a distant thought; He will be the central figure in our lives personally and together forever. Beyond all precious and perfect human relationships we will enjoy, we will enjoy His presence, real and tangible, forever. Though we were to travel to the furthest reaches of our new world, we would always be in His presence, speaking with Him, listening to Him. He will be more real and present to us then than our thoughts are to us now.

Which Jesus Shall We See?

One of the mysteries of heaven is that our Lord has been revealed in different ways in the Scriptures, particularly in the Revelation. His appearances are amazing and wondrous—but also confusing. That these are appearances of our Lord is indisputable, yet they are not only different from our earthly concepts of Him as the Nazarene but also different from other revelations of Him in Scripture and prophetic passages.

Our Lord in His humanity was transfigured before the disciples while on earth, displaying His glory in a way His physical body at that time could not contain (Matthew 17:1–2). His glory can never be contained in a human form, even a glorified human form, so we should expect to see different manifestations of His glory in different ways in heaven.

Some have seen manifestations of His glory, as in the God/man Jesus, but His human form could never fully express His eternal and infinite glory. We have seen accommodations only for sinful eyes. But one day we will finally see Him as He is in His presence (Matthew 5:8). We shall see God. We shall finally *be able* to see God. No longer will we have to make do with the fire by night, cloud by day, burning bush, and other lesser manifestations of His glory. He will finally be able to reveal Himself to us just as He really is.

In Revelation 1:13–18 John sees Jesus as someone "like a son of man," but his description is stunningly symbolic. In Revelation 2:18, Jesus is describing Himself to the church at Thyatira as one "whose eyes are like blazing fire and whose feet are like burnished bronze." In Revelation 4:2–3, we see someone sitting on a throne in heaven described with "the appearance of jasper and carnelian." In Revelation 5:5–6 our Lord is described as "a Lamb, looking as if it had been slain, standing in the center of the throne, encircled by the four living creatures and the elders. He had seven horns and seven eyes, which are the seven spirits of God sent out into all the earth." Revelation 19:11–16 offers a further description that inspires and confuses at the same time.

All of these appearances of our Lord lead us to the natural question: Which Jesus shall we see? Will we see the Lord who appeared to the twelve in the upper room, or the one who appears so dramatically in Revelation?

We can say with certainty that our Lord isn't limited to any one appearance, though He never ceases to have His glorified human form. To limit deity is to deny deity. Furthermore, we can understand that many of these appearances are designed to express truths about our Lord in a visible, symbolic way. Jesus appearing to John as a Lamb that was slain clearly identifies not only Jesus' person in His crucifixion and in prophetic Scripture, but also His mission to bring us back to God our Father through His atoning sacrifice. Obviously our Lord wanted us to think of those aspects of His divine nature and work as we listened to the Revelation He was giving to John.

Albert Barnes wrote, "In that future abode he [the believer] will be permitted to know all that is to be known in those worlds that shine upon his path by day or by night; all that is to be known in the character of their Maker, and the principles of his government; all that is to be known of the glorious plan of redemption; all that is to be known of the reasons why sin and woe were permitted to enter this beautiful world."[1]

Our Lord will undoubtedly express Himself to us in many ways throughout all eternity, teaching us new things about Himself through every manifestation, yet He will never cease to be flesh and bone as well. The question of how He will appear to us forever is a source of great anticipation and a subject of eternal learning.

Unhindered Access

Today, no matter how close we feel to our Lord, we still feel a profound sense of distance between us. Though we know He is intimately acquainted with us and guiding us, without visual confirmation of that fact we have to accept it by faith. There are moments when we fervently wish we could just look Him in the eye and ask Him precisely what He wants us to do and be. One day we *will* see Him.

Furthermore, we won't be allowed a few one-on-one moments with our creator, like Dorothy had with the Wizard of Oz when she finally reached the Emerald City. We will have unhindered access to Him forever. No need to make appointments fifty years ahead. To say it more clearly, He is Immanuel, God with *you*—forever.

It is only with the greatest difficulty that we imagine God being so near, so present, so tangible in every way that our eternity will be most affected by that one fact. We won't have to "check-in" with God, for He will always be present—not as He is today, through His invisible Spirit indwelling us. He will be ever present *to* us, ever present *with* us, and that won't be intimidating, frightening, or annoying—it will be the single greatest source of our joy.

I have a beautiful wife named Annette. She is my closest and dearest friend, the greatest human love of my life. I am closer to her than to any other human being. But in heaven my greatest relationship, my most intimate relationship, will be with God Himself. So will Annette's. So will yours. It will not in any way minimize our dear human relationships, for we will all feel the same. We will finally be complete in Him, loving Him the way we always wanted to, but were never able to, on earth.

You will more often, more naturally, more intimately speak to your Lord in heaven than anyone you loved on earth. You will come before Him in perfect holiness and absolute confidence; in fact, you will never leave Him to have to return again. His presence and glory will fill the whole new earth and new heavens.

We will no longer have to take His omnipresence as an article of faith—it will be our new reality. We will simply never be out of His immediate presence, never tiring of our intimate relationship with Him. In our relationships with one another, we will be in relationship with Him, each of us a unique expression of His glory to each other, and yet this new relationship in His presence will not erase our identities or personalities.

God Wants Us in His Presence

Do we really appreciate the fact that God has always wanted us to live in His immediate presence? It was always His desire. Have we thought about that? So often we can feel that God is willing to allow us into His presence, but do we see in Scripture that this was what God created us for and desired from the very beginning?

Your creator is not a disinterested deity who has left you alone to try to find Him. He is the one who brought you into being, uniquely from all other beings, to glorify Himself. He has always wanted you to be in His immediate presence. Heaven will be the fulfillment not only of our longings but the eternal will and plan of Him who loves us most dearly.

God did not make you like a factory makes cookies, millions upon millions, all the same, cranked out of the same mold thoughtlessly. The perfect, eternal God made you with perfect love and infinite knowledge and wisdom to declare His glory forever in a unique and special way.

When I got married, I wanted to spend all my time with Annette. I hated being separated from her. It is the natural desire of a groom for his bride; so it should come as no surprise that God speaks of the church, us, as His bride. Yes, if that thought hasn't quite gotten through yet, we will be married in heaven!

Married in Heaven

Contrary to what you have probably heard, we will be married in heaven—not to our spouses but to the Lord Himself. We will finally become fully His, the object of His eternal love and devotion.

Human marriage was always meant to be but a foreshadow of things to come. Paul calls the relationship between Jesus and the church "a profound mystery" (Ephesians 5:32–33) but makes clear that it relates to what he is really talking about—Christ and the church. The Scriptures reveal that we, the church, are indeed His eternal bride—the focus of His eternal love (2 Corinthians 11:1–6; Revelation 19:7; Revelation 21). We don't think about the implications of that deeply enough.

Marriage was designed not only for procreation but also for intimacy (Genesis 2:8). In the marriage relationship as God designed it (not as it is often experienced, sadly), we have wonderful intimacy with someone who loves us dearly and who wants only our best. It is a uniquely exclusive relationship between one man and one woman where they each turn their romantic love and energy in only one direction—toward their spouse. We desire this exclusive love, this special feeling of being the single and only romantic love of the other. It fulfills a deep yearning within us of belonging and intimacy.

In heaven, in His presence forever, we will finally eat the banquet for which all human marriages and loves were but hors d'oeuvres. We will not miss having the one relationship through which we find our life and fulfillment, for we shall finally experience the real thing with our Lord.

As an infinite being He can simultaneously be intimate and present with all of us. Furthermore, there will be an intimacy God has with us that will be different from all others, and that will be the fulfillment of our original creation.

On earth others may not value our differences or uniqueness, as other people just look at them from a human perspective. But each one of us was made uniquely in His image to glorify Him, and there is something inside each of us—in our personalities, hearts, and minds—that does not correspond exactly to anyone else. We each add a different tone and hue to the praise we offer Him. None is better; each is unique.

External Signs of His Love

We are told in Revelation 22:4 that in the marvelous New Jerusalem, the city of God, we will see His face, and His name will be on our foreheads. The ring as an expression of marriage will be replaced by a mark on our foreheads, and we must not think of this mark as something crude or ugly, like the stamp of a number or a tattoo. It will be a mark of beauty and precious to us. It will be an external sign of His love and care for us. (Some feel this mark is merely symbolic of our Lord's love and relationship to us, which may be true. If so, God is telling us in a unique way how much we will mean to Him forever.)

In Revelation 2:17 we are told that to each one who overcomes (every true believer) will be given a white stone with a new name written on it, known only to him who receives it.

George MacDonald articulates this idea so beautifully: "God's name for a man must be the expression of His own idea of the man, that being whom He had in His thought when He began to make the child, and whom He kept in His thought through the long process of creation which went to realize the idea. To tell the name is to seal the success. What does it mean that the name is a secret 'which no one knows except him who receives it?' That with every man He has a secret—the secret of a new name. In every man there is loneliness, an inner chamber of peculiar life into which God only can enter. There is a chamber also (O God, humble and accept my speech)—a chamber in God Himself, into which none can enter but the one, the individual, the peculiar man—out of which chamber that man has to bring revelation and strength for his brethren. This is that for which he was made—to reveal the secret things of the Father."[2]

Joni Eareckson Tada writes, "Only in heaven—the birthplace of our identity—will we find out who we truly are. Our true identity will unfold in the new name God will give us. You will not only find what was irretrievably lost, but when you receive it—your new name, your true identity, you will be a thousand times more yourself than the sum total of all those nuances, gestures, and inside subtleties that defined the earthbound 'you.' On earth you may think you fully blossomed, but heaven will reveal that you barely budded.

"What's more, you will be like none other in heaven. The fact that no one else has your name shows how utterly unique you are to God. You touch His heart in a way no one else can. It is a royal seal of His individual love on you.

"You have a specific place marked in heaven—in God's heart—which fits you and you alone. In heaven you will reflect Him like the facet of a diamond, and people will say to you, 'I love seeing that part of God in you.'

"United in perfect praise and love, we will finally and fully discover who we are, where we belong, and what God destined us to do—and we will have all of eternity to be and do that very thing."[3]

Sometimes in our world we struggle with the love of God toward us. We know intellectually that He loves us, but if we admitted the truth, we don't often feel that love except in faint hints and elusive emotions that refuse to stay and comfort us perpetually. In the same way that those who are color blind are aware that colors surround them on all sides, though they can't see them, so the myriad ways God shows His love toward us are equally imperceptible. In heaven I am convinced that one of our greatest and continuing joys will be that we will be able to see clearly the ways God showed His love toward us that we were blinded to on earth.

There we will know His love more clearly and certainly than we know anything else.

We won't just be able to know we are loved—it will be the air we breathe, the eternal atmosphere, the natural law of the new earth and new heavens. Best of all, we won't have to earn it; we will simply be able, finally, to receive His great love completely unfiltered.

It will not be that in His presence He will love us more than He does now, for God is love and He never changes (Malachi 3:6; 1 John 4:7–8), but that finally we will be able to fully recognize and receive His love without any interference of sin, weakness, or ignorance.

How much thought have you given to the fact that one day you will be face to face with your creator? It is impossible to prepare for heaven rightly unless we have seriously considered this reality. We will see Him just as He is. The better country will forever be the place that He lives with us. But that is only one part of the wonder of what is to come. For as we will finally see Him as He truly is, we will also finally be revealed as the person God always intended us to be.

When God perfects us, we will be forever different as well. We've spoken a great deal about what heaven will be like, but a pressing question for us is what will we be like—*forever*?

The journey continues.

CHAPTER EIGHT

Transformation . . . *Complete!*

But we all, with unveiled face, beholding as in a mirror the glory of the Lord, *are being transformed* into the same image from glory to glory, just as from the Lord, the Spirit (2 Corinthians 3:18 NASB, emphasis added).

For all of my Christian experience, I have sought to become the man God would have me to be. And always, I have fallen short. Though positionally I am seated in the heavenly realms (Ephesians 2:6–7) with Christ Jesus, and His righteousness has been given to me (Romans 3:21–22; 4:5–6; 5:17; 9:30; 2 Corinthians 5:21), practically I'm always going to be a work-in-progress on earth. Though I know He loves and accepts me through the work of Jesus on my behalf, I experience regret over my constant failures, even though I realize that I'm forgiven.

This leads to a wonderfully important part of heaven—the fact that it will be the place and time when all that God originally planned for us will be fulfilled. In our world we have a popular motto made famous by the song "I've Gotta Be Me." We want to be proud of who we are and what we have accomplished on earth. But the most we can celebrate here on earth is the marred image of God in man. In an ironic way, none of us is really who we were meant to be. All we really are is the sinful distortion of what God intended, and just saying that raises the hackles of some people.

We are victims of spiritual leprosy—born with the disease that disfigures and will ultimately destroy us. Never having been around anyone without the disease, we could call ourselves normal. But when Jesus came into our world and lived among us, we finally experienced someone born without the disease. Suddenly our disfigurement became apparent, and we either shrank away in shame or struck out at Him in resentment.

It is only fitting that when we finally see Him as He is, it will dramatically change us. Somewhere in the infinite divine wisdom and foreknowledge of

God, the real Dan Schaeffer, the Dan Schaeffer who will live forever, exists in the mind and will of God, and that person will be restored. Paul wrote in 1 Corinthians 13:9–10, 12: "For we know in part and we prophesy in part, but when perfection comes, the imperfect disappears . . . Now we see but a poor reflection as in a mirror; then we shall see face to face. Now I know in part; then I shall know fully, even as I am fully known."

Later Paul added, "And we, who with unveiled faces all reflect the Lord's glory, are being transformed into His likeness with ever-increasing glory" (2 Corinthians 3:18).

There is so much in me today that resists the person that God wants to make me. He wants me to meet and interact with people; I want to remain safely isolated. He wants me to step out and attempt something in faith; I want to draw back in fear. I want to change an attitude, a habit, a thought pattern—but every time I try I realize I don't want it badly enough to give up the sinful behavior. He wants to put His heart in me, and I resist.

One day, all that is in me that resists the good—that would complete my transformation into the image of Christ—will be removed. I will for the first time in my life be completely and entirely good. I will breathe my first truly perfect human breath, for that is what I was always designed for. The wooden soldier will come alive; the fairytale will come true. Pinocchio will become, finally, a real boy.

The transformation will be, quite literally, heavenly. It almost sounds too good to be true, like a fairytale. But that is because we have forgotten that this was God's plan all along—to repair what happened in the garden. Put simply, this wasn't the way we were designed to live; we were designed to live without the ruining influence of sin.

What Will I Be Like?

How different will I be from who I am now—and yet, also, how alike? It is an incredible thought that I will finally discover the real Dan Schaeffer, the person God always intended me to become. Many parts of the old Dan—my personality, my passions, my gifts and unique interests—will, I believe, remain—but they will undergo a metamorphosis far more dramatic than that demonstrated by the caterpillar that emerges from his transformation as a beautiful butterfly.

It is interesting how we spend so much of our lives wishing we were someone else. This is precisely because we are all so dissatisfied with ourselves. We wish we were as brave as our greatest heroes, as accomplished as those whose success we admire and envy, as talented as those artists we most appreciate, as intelligent as those thinkers we most respect, as tall or beautiful as our world's most beautiful people. Most magazines, books, and movies cater to our desire to be different from who we really are, allowing us to live out adventures and fantasies vicariously through fictional characters. We indulge in these activities precisely because we desire to be quite different from who we are at times.

This is the part of that better country that we think about far too little. I have noticed that the older I get, the wearier I am of the old me. In many ways I am so far from our Lord's image in actual practice that I long for that part of heaven where I will be changed forever. Earthly transformation is wearying work. I find that I am weary of my sin, weary of my failures, weary of my ignorance, weary of my shortcomings, weary of my sinful nature that always chooses sin first, and only with great effort is countered by my new nature.

I am bone weary of discovering new layers of my sin nature the closer I draw to Christ. The light of His Spirit upon the inner parts of my heart is both enlightening and depressing. I tire of the struggle, of the temptations, and want eternal rest from that. Like a heavy weight you put on your shoulders and carry, the longer you carry it the heavier it feels, and you look forward to that moment of relief you know will come when you can, finally, put it down for good. You try to imagine what that moment will feel like, but you can't. It has to be experienced.

I agree with C. S. Lewis when he wrote, "If you think of this world as a place intended simply for our happiness, you find it quite intolerable: think of it as a place of training and correction and it's not so bad."[1]

What Was I Really Created For?

It will not be until God has made me new in heart, mind, and body that I will be able to understand or fulfill that marvelous design He has for me. God did not create me for a short seventy- to eighty-year life span. It is foolish to believe that this life will reveal to me His plan for my life in entirety. I was created for eternity. I do not yet have a clue what He has planned for me to do that will both glorify Him and fulfill me in ways I can't imagine—forever!

The gifts, passions, and abilities that God has given and revealed to you are, and will remain for your entire earthly existence, in embryo. Isn't that an exciting thought?

We can often feel sad and regretful that our lives never lived up to the grandiose dreams we had as children. There are moments when we wonder what might have been if only our lives had been different. Those thoughts lead quickly to despondence. These are not the thoughts of those who understand that this world, as wonderful as it can be, is not our only opportunity to realize the ambitions God created for us.

Earthly ambition is not a sin, but it can be a terrible disappointment when it's not achieved. We can feel that our one and only chance to really amount to something has been lost. Often loss, accidents, unforeseen circumstances, missed opportunities, and other things seem to conspire to snatch opportunity from our grasp. Our world is filled with disappointed dreamers. We never fulfilled our potential—or at least what *we felt* was our potential.

Even if we are one of the "fortunate ones" who achieved our dreams, we find that the promised fulfillment falls far short of what we expected. Fulfillment simply can't be fully experienced in a sinful world—like trying to enjoy your favorite dessert when you are nauseated, the bad destroys the pleasure of the good.

But one day your God-given abilities, talents, and passions will be perfected to such a degree that you could not recognize them in their former strength. And those gifts will be yours forever, a part of you that God always had in mind to bloom in you forever. None of us, even the most accomplished among us, has ever experienced anything but the bare budding of our God-given talents and gifts.

In the better country that all changes.

Your Best Days Are Ahead of You, Not Behind You

Not only will our talents, passions, and abilities be perfected, but far more importantly, our ambitions will be perfected as well. Everything we do, make, or accomplish will be unto His glory—forever! We won't have to remember to try to stay humble. We will fully recognize what our gifts are for and who gave them to us.

Your greatest accomplishments, your most fulfilling moments, your most beautiful creations lie ahead of you in the better country. What joy will be ours when we are able to do, to be, and to create things we couldn't even dream of doing, being, or creating here on earth as we enter into the inheritance that is ours in Christ! The *new you* is part of your inheritance!

Your greatest moments as a Christian are always ahead of you if you are alive on earth in this world. It is the promise of heaven that allows us to let go of the things people in our world hold to so tightly. People are taught that they go around only once in life, so they have to grab everything they can while they can. They are driven to possess, to acquire, accumulate, and compare—for only then do they feel they can find fulfillment.

They sense that time is running out, which pushes them even harder. They are in a frenetic chase for the end of the rainbow. In this world you can only chase the rainbow—it is in the better country that the rainbow ends.

Today we are preparing for heaven. The greatest part of your life—indeed, the rest of your life—which never ends, will be ample time to be all God planned for you to be.

I would love a new perfect body, a new perfect mind, a new perfect attitude and outlook, and a new set of perfect talents and abilities. Wouldn't you? Again, within ourselves we experience that "holy discontentment" we spoke of earlier. As we look at others we are reminded only of our deficiencies. We're too short, too fat, too old, too young, too dumb, too smart, too poor, too average, too inferior—ad infinitum.

What will it be like one day to live in complete joy and perfect contentment in who I am—in full view of others and their unique and perfect creations? We can't imagine thinking of ourselves without being acutely aware of our faults and shortcomings since we're trained to see ourselves in light of others.

In those few moments in my past when I was happy with myself and what I had accomplished on earth, my heart was quickly tempted to turn it to sin. A success is too frequently victimized by my sin nature. What will it be like one day to be fulfilled in every way with every part of my being—to go far beyond simple contentment—and be filled with unending joy in the person God has made of me? Furthermore, there will be nothing to stir pride in me, for I will simply be a new creation—not a "pulled-myself-up-by-my-own-bootstraps" story. I will finally be who *God* always intended me to be.

This is the final part of our salvation that began with our forgiveness, our confession of faith, and our justification[2] by Christ. The appropriate doctrinal term for this miracle of final and eternal transformation is *sanctification*. The term *sanctification* refers to being set aside from sin unto God. Yet sanctification in the Bible has three key aspects: the past, the present, and the future.

If you have believed in Jesus and are trusting in Him and what He did for you on the cross for your salvation, you have been saved in the past from the *penalty* of sin (eternal death, hell). Today you are being saved from the *power* of sin, resulting in holiness. But one day you and I will be saved from the *presence* of sin itself. I will undergo a transformation of my being so cataclysmic that every microscopic vestige of sin will leave my entire being and never be able to find a home there again. I will not only be cleansed of all sin but forever become immune to it, though sin's presence will forever be destroyed as well. Sin, in the better country, won't just be missing from our lives and our environment; it will be removed as a reality.

Those words can sound so ethereal and pious, and yet the implications are incredible.

What Will It Be Like?

Though we spoke of this earlier, we can't dwell too much on how we will be changed in the better country. What will life be like when I no longer have to hide my feelings or thoughts from others because they are evil or stupid or immature? What would relationships be like for me if I never had to watch what I said or choose my words carefully so as not to offend? What would relationships be like when I could with full freedom say exactly what I mean and mean exactly what I say because every thought I had and every word I uttered were perfectly truthful, completely accurate, and full of love? It will be life in the better country!

As incredible as it sounds to me, one day I will simply be unable to offend either by word or action. I will speak truthfully and perfectly as easily as I take a breath here on earth. It will be more natural and effortless than the beating of my heart. One of my greatest joys is the knowledge that I will never again be able to hurt someone by something I say or do or by something I left unsaid or undone.

I will never again be insecure about my identity. I will never again have to make an excuse for some thoughtless statement or action or try to pretend to be something I'm not or try desperately to conceal what I really am. I will never again want something I shouldn't or be attracted to things I shouldn't. Everything I choose, everything I say, everything I do, and everything I want will be good and right and holy. I will want only what Christ has designed me to want, and it will be good. And I will be happier than imagination can conceive.

And unlike today, I will truly desire the right things. Today I can desire in my spiritual man to be holy but still struggle with desires that are evil and destructive. Everything that I desire in the better country will not only be good for me, and allowed, but more delightful to me than any delight I've experienced on earth.

Jesus said, " 'But the things that proceed out of the mouth come from the heart, and those defile the man. For out of the heart come evil thoughts, murders, adulteries, fornications, thefts, false witness, slanders. These are the things which defile the man'" (Matthew 15:18–20 NASB). He makes it clear that the only way to change a man is to change him completely from the inside out, starting with the heart. When our hearts have been restored to their final condition of Christlike character, only good things will come out of it—*forever!*

That was the promise of the Old Testament, that one day God would change our hearts: "And I will give them one heart, and put a new spirit within them. And I will take the heart of stone out of their flesh and give them a heart of flesh, that they may walk in My statutes and keep My ordinances and do them. Then they will be My people, and I shall be their God" (Ezekiel 11:19–20 NASB).

"Moreover, I will give you a new heart and put a new spirit within you; and I will remove the heart of stone from your flesh and give you a heart of flesh. I will put My Spirit within you and cause you to walk in

My statutes, and you will be careful to observe My ordinances" (Ezekiel 36:26–27 NASB).

We can only imagine.

The New Me

Mentally: A Transformed Mind

It sounds silly even to say this, and those who are younger will not fully appreciate this because their minds are young, sharp, and alert—but in the better country I will never again try to think of the right word and not be able to remember it. Never again will my mind go fuzzy or simply be unable to understand something because it's way beyond my intelligence.

How often over the years have I felt stupid (especially in math classes) or inept (trying to figure out mechanical devices) or unable to grasp concepts that come so easily to others. For it won't be just my heart that will be renewed and perfected—but also my mind. "*Be made new in the attitude of your minds*; and to put on the new self, created to be like God in true righteousness and holiness" (Ephesians 4:23–24, emphasis added). How desperately do our minds need to be renewed?

"This is the covenant I will make with them after that time, says the Lord. I will put my laws in their hearts, and I will write them on their minds" (Hebrews 10:16). It is clear that these wonderful actions (writing His laws on our hearts and on our minds) are going to be accomplished *for us* by God.

Paul prays for the Colossians, "that their hearts may be encouraged, having been knit together in love, and attaining to all the wealth that comes from the full assurance of understanding, resulting in a true knowledge of God's mystery, that is, Christ Himself, *in whom are hidden all the treasures of wisdom and knowledge*" (Colossians 2:2–3 NASB, emphasis added). We will gain all these treasures of wisdom and knowledge. It is safe to say we could not possibly understand them or assimilate them all now. Our minds, affected by sin, no longer have the capacity to comprehend all these treasures any more than a thimble could contain the oceans of the world.

Paul writes to the Corinthian church: "Now I know in part; *then I shall know fully, even as I am fully known*" (1 Corinthians 13:12, emphasis added). One day we will know *fully*! Our minds will clearly understand everything that is knowable to us. Today I can know some things, but other things my mind can't assimilate. One day that won't be true.

Our minds struggle enough trying to understand all there is to know in this world. When we think of all that is knowable in science, mathematics, history, art, philosophy, technology, politics, and so many more subjects, we are overwhelmed. It is virtually impossible for human beings, even the most intelligent and learned among us, to fully know all that is in even their limited field of expertise.

When it comes to the knowledge of God, an infinite subject, we are even more inadequate. This does not mean we don't know the truth about God, for He has revealed it to us in Scripture, but that revelation of Himself was tailored to our imperfect minds. This doesn't mean we have wrong information, only that what we have been told is limited. The truth about our God could hardly be contained in thousands of books on the subject! Our finite, imperfect minds could no more understand all there is to know about God than a baby in the womb could comprehend all the galaxies in the universe. There are many truths our present condition and experience preclude us from being able to understand.

Even the Scriptures themselves, though they are inspired by God, are extremely limited in what they share with us. Paul makes this clear in 1 Corinthians 13:8–10: "Love never fails; but if there are gifts of prophecy, they will be done away; if there are tongues, they will cease; if there is knowledge, it will be done away. For we know in part and we prophesy in part; but when the perfect comes, the partial will be done away" (NASB).

When Paul says that knowledge and prophecy will be done away with, he doesn't mean that knowledge will no longer exist but that what we will know will be so far superior to what has been revealed to us that our present knowledge will no longer be our point of reference. When children finally really learn how to ride a bicycle, they no longer need the training wheels, and although the training wheels still work fine, the parents remove them and leave them behind.

Paul says we know in part and we prophesy in part. We can share only what we have been told, and we have been told only part of the whole truth there is to know. But one day, when we see Him and are transformed in our minds, we shall know fully. Not only will a whole new dimension of life we never imagined be made accessible to us, allowing us to know fully (like the baby who is finally born and leaves the womb to begin exploring the new world it has entered), but our minds will finally be able to assimilate it all.

We will finally *be able* to be filled with the knowledge of God in all its dimensions. The knowledge of this present world, as vast as it all is, will be a drop in the ocean of the knowledge we will gain at our transformation. And to fully comprehend this knowledge will take a mind made new by God.

The idea that one day I will be able to understand my Lord so much better—His will, His Word, His being—is exciting. I will need a new mind, a transformed mind, to think thoughts that honor God and to receive and understand thoughts from God.

Today I can think such puny erroneous ideas about God. My mind is afflicted with so much bad information and influenced by my cultural and experiential backgrounds. My thinking can be illogical, fallible, incomplete, fragmented, and unable to grasp His wisdom. I am willing by faith to believe what my mind does not always fully understand, but one day I will be able to understand what today I can only believe. One day I will grasp better the tri-unity of God, His marvelous incarnation, His resurrection, the miracle of creation, and so many more things that today I must accept by faith alone.

Today we look at our physical world, and all we have are questions. It is like trying to put together a thousand-piece puzzle with only ten pieces. How could such an amazing act of creation have occurred? How could God create out of nothing, by just speaking creation into existence? How could this universe of planets, galaxies, and stars have been designed to work as perfectly as it does? How does our body work? We're still trying to discover the answer to that. How could God actually become a man and yet still be God? These questions and a thousand more nag our minds because we have no good answer. Our minds can't get around them.

We understand the power of a nuclear bomb and can give testimony to its destructive capacity—but few truly understand how it works. In the same way we can observe God's creation and works without really understanding how it all happened.

This is not to say that I will ever truly understand all about God—for He will forever be infinite and I will forever be finite. To be made perfect is not to be made divine, for to be made anything is to be a creation. Only the divine has no beginning and no end. I will never have the capacity to understand everything about Him, but one day I will see and understand so much more about Him. I will be in awe forever as my mind grasps more and more of His perfect being.

We will be able to glorify God and honor Him with our minds far more in eternity when the clouds have lifted and the cobwebs have been brushed away from our minds.

Physically: Bodies Built for Eternity

We must speak, if only briefly, about the new physical me. In the better country we will exist in glorified bodies of flesh and bone. That part, at least, will be familiar to us. We have flesh and bone bodies now, but that is where the similarity ends.

Our present bodies have a built-in obsolescence plan of seventy to eighty years on average. Even now, as I write these words, my eyesight and hearing are fading, my mind is not quite as sharp as it used to be, my memory is unreliable, my back prone to go out, my hair graying (what's left of it), my strength lessening, my wrinkles increasing, and creaks are multiplying; youthful energy is a fading memory. There have been moments on earth where I felt so strong and vital and energetic that I could hardly sit still. Sadly, those memories are faded now.

But the new me will include a body designed to last, in fact *to thrive*, forever! That mere fact is awe-inspiring. I have often stood gazing up at Half Dome and El Capitan in Yosemite National Park. These two stone monoliths rising thousands of feet above the ground are the pictures of permanence. Yet given enough time and wear, even these rocks will crumble as the effects of cold and wind and rain take their toll. It would take hundreds of thousands, even millions, of years, but given enough time it would happen. Simply stated, nothing in our world is indestructible.

But one day I will inhabit a body that will be created so that eternity can't wear it down or in any way weaken it. Your glorified body and mine will be infinitely more permanent and indestructible than Half Dome and El Capitan. Strength, energy, vitality, and agility will be part of my physical inheritance. The amazing truth is that I would need just such a body to enjoy this better country forever.

Bodies that hurt, that fail us, that deteriorate over time and are vulnerable to a plethora of dangers will become immortal. We will be sons and daughters of the living God, and our physical inheritance is only one small part of that.

It is instructive to think of how much our physical condition affects our mental, emotional, and spiritual conditions. Pain and sickness are disheartening, and they can drain us of optimism and hope. When no relief is in sight, we find our faith being stretched and, at times, weakened.

But one day it will not be so. Your body will never grow weary or sick or weak or inhibit your enjoyment and fulfillment of life in any way. Just the opposite. Your sense of physical well-being will be part of your joy and fulfillment forever. I have recently begun running again to get in shape and yet am painfully aware that my aging body can no longer do what my younger body could. My desire no longer equals my ability. In heaven there will be joy again in our physical glorified bodies as they will be able to do far beyond what our physical earthly bodies could ever do.

In short, our body's best days are also ahead of it. What will my new body be able to do? Where will my new body be able to go, and what will it be able to experience there that it never could here? Our Lord's glorified body (a pre-runner to ours) on earth was not constrained by gravity or inhibited by solid walls or any of the other constraints normal earthly bodies face. Our new bodies will be perfect compliments to our new hearts and minds.

My new body will be perfectly in sync with its perfect environment. No longer will certain foods disagree with me or will certain things in the environment cause bad reactions like allergies. Our bodies will be in their perfect environment. We often use that phrase *perfect natural environment* for a fish in water, a bird in the sky, or a worm in the earth. But that isn't really true. There is danger, sickness, risk, and death in every "perfect natural environment" here on earth. Our bodies are not safe here. In the better country we will enter a world where our perfect bodies will compliment the perfect environment.

As J. Oswald Sanders says, "We will have bodies fit for the full life of God to indwell and express itself forever. We will be able to eat but will not need to. We will be able to move rapidly through space and matter. We will be ageless and not know pain, tears, sorrow, sickness or death. We will have bodies of splendor. In a promise to the Old Testament saints, the Lord compared our glorious bodies to the shining of the moon and stars (Daniel 12:3)."[3]

It is with new bodies, new eyes, new arms, legs, noses, ears, and fingers that we will experience the better country that awaits us. We will explore our new world with these new bodies. How wonderful it will be! Paul talks about our earthly bodies and our heavenly bodies in 1 Corinthians 15:49 when he writes, "And just as we have borne the likeness of the earthly man, so shall we bear the likeness of the man from heaven."

Emotionally: A New Heart

Sometimes I feel so happy I can barely contain myself. I just want to jump and shout. I live for those moments, for they are rare. I can be mildly happy frequently or even for long stretches, but ecstatically happy—happy beyond the ability to properly express it, happy that can bring me to tears—those times are rare.

Ironically, only a short time later I can also grow sad. Perpetual joy, the elusive fountain of emotional fulfillment, is simply not available for us on earth, despite what the advertisers try to tell us.

There are times when I am troubled or worried and not even quite sure why. My emotions respond to the multiple stimuli they receive both outwardly and inwardly. We can't always know why we are feeling certain emotions because they can be responding to neglected or forgotten experiences. Yet emotions are a powerful part of who each one of us is. Our unique personalities demonstrate our emotions uniquely. Some of us wear our emotions on our sleeves; our feelings are out there for all to see. Others of us keep our most powerful and personal emotions cloaked—yet we feel them just as strongly as those who express them more easily.

Unfortunately, our emotions often lead us into decisions and actions that take us away from God and His will for us. Too often in life I've trusted my emotions to guide me and ended up disappointed. In being made new, being prepared to live forever in the better country, I will experience an emotional transformation to coincide with the transformation of my mind and heart. Or, perhaps more accurately, my new heart and mind will only provoke the right emotions within me.

However it comes about, the new Dan Schaeffer will finally experience appropriate emotions and respond perfectly emotionally. I will finally feel everything I'm supposed to feel about life, myself, other people, and, far more importantly, about God.

There are times when other things can make me feel so pleasant and happy (success, achievements, beauty, wealth) that I am tempted to worship those things more than God. There are times when watching a sunset or being with good friends and family can "feel" more powerful and enticing to me than the way I feel about God at the moment. One day things will be different. I will feel exactly what I should feel at every moment with exactly the appropriate intensity and never, for one moment, feel ashamed of my emotional response.

What will it be like for us to know exactly how we should feel? Only our Lord ever experienced that. Emotions that so often confuse us were clear and natural for Him in His perfect humanity. But in His time in our sinful world He had to experience the most powerful negative emotions any person has ever experienced of grief, despair, loss, and betrayal. In the better country, part of our inheritance is that none of these negative emotions will be possible.

We will be capable of more powerful emotions than we can even imagine here on earth, but they will be responding to perfect and wondrous stimuli. We will finally know what to do with our emotions, something we aren't usually sure of here on earth. No longer will we try to hold our emotions in check or bottle them up, afraid of what others will say or think. No longer will we have to try to hide feelings we have toward others for fear they might be misunderstood.

We will finally feel what we are supposed to feel! We will be like Him, for we shall see Him as He is. Out of a new heart will come powerfully perfect emotional responses.

Spiritually: Perfect Service

The greatest news we could hear is that the new me will be able finally and fully and completely to serve, honor, and glorify our Lord forever—

perfectly. That which only the good angels can do now will be our new birthright.

Never again will I question or hesitate to do His will. I won't simply be able to serve Him perfectly—nothing in heaven will bring me greater joy. I will find perfect words to glorify Him and will honor Him by reacting perfectly toward His other children.

Imagine how much time you've spent in this life seeking His will against the strong current of your own sin and ignorance. But in the better country the current of life will be perfectly righteous, and you and the current of life will finally run in the same direction. Godliness and holiness will be as natural as breathing.

I won't just know His will in general; I will know His will for me, Dan Schaeffer. When I speak of Him I will always be right, for I will know Him as He is. There will be no "keep out" signs in the better country, for there will be nothing that is out of bounds and nothing in us that would desire anything out of bounds. I will finally have His heart in me and forever only want to please Him—for that will be my greatest desire.

Though that desire resides in me today, the fulfillment does not. But the wind is changing; eternal spring is not far off. We are the buds of the new world. One day we will bloom.

There is so much more to our eternal inheritance than we ever imagined. Today we would desperately love to start being the kind of people Jesus is going to make of us. The new you will be better by far than anything you have ever imagined.

Every day you are closer to this reality. Our transformation has already begun.

The better country is drawing nearer every day to you. Are you prepared?

The journey continues.

PART FOUR

Heavenly Preparation

The goal we were always meant to pursue

CHAPTER NINE

Preparing for Heaven

We are afraid that heaven is a bribe, and that if we make it our goal we shall no longer be disinterested. It is not so. Heaven offers nothing that a mercenary soul can desire. It is safe to tell the pure in heart that they shall see God, for only the pure in heart want to.[1]   —C. S. Lewis

We have spent many chapters talking about the nature of heaven, but if you are now convinced of its majesty, reality, and imminence, there remains one great issue—*preparing* for it. The question is not *whether* you are preparing for heaven but *how* you are preparing for heaven.

A truly sad thought is that the Bible makes it very clear that it is quite possible to enter heaven, to truly be saved, but have nothing of value to commend your life.

While the Bible teaches that the Christian will never be the object of God's wrathful judgment (Romans 8:1), there will be a day of judgment in the future for reward; that is, a day will come when we will receive rewards for all that we have done for God. This is often called the judgment seat of Christ. While there is another judgment at the end of time, the great white throne judgment (Revelation 20:11–15), believers won't be judged here because our sins were judged already on Calvary. At the judgment seat of Christ that will take place when Christ returns (Matthew 16:27; Revelation 22:12), we will be rewarded not only for what we have *done* for Him but also for what we have *become* for Him.

"For we must all appear before the judgment seat of Christ, that each one may receive what is due him for the things done while in the body, whether good or bad" (2 Corinthians 5:10).

"Each man's work will become evident; for the day will show it because it is to be revealed with fire, and the fire itself will test the quality of each man's work. If any man's work which he has built on it remains, he will receive a reward. If any man's work is burned up, he will suffer loss; but he himself will be saved, yet so as through fire" (1 Corinthians 3:13–15 NASB).

Most frequently, when people hear the exhortation to prepare for heaven, they translate that into, "Get your affairs in order; death is around the corner." But the Bible never talks about preparing for heaven in those terms. We are urged to spend our whole lives preparing for heaven with all our energy and resources (Matthew 6:19–21; Luke 12:33; 18:29–30; 1 Timothy 6:19, 20). We are, in fact, urged to focus our lives on things above. Our earthly lives are not simply an interlude before "the real thing."

Paul reminds the Colossian Christians to "keep seeking the things above, where Christ is, seated at the right hand of God. Set your mind on the things above, not on the things that are on earth. For you have died and your life is hidden with Christ in God. When Christ, who is our life, is revealed, then you also will be revealed with Him in glory" (Colossians 3:1–4 NASB).

Why does Paul say this? He says it because he knows how easy it is to stop seeking the things above and to set our minds only, or primarily, on earthly things. To live out this command requires a complete change in our thinking and daily activity, not simply a momentary reflective insight.

The Goal

It seems such a strange command that we treat it as hyperbole. Preparing for heaven is far more than keeping the idea in the back of your mind that one day you will answer for everything you've done. Preparing for heaven is nothing less than accepting a radical new paradigm for living.

- This earthly life, as real as it feels, is only temporary.
- The next life is the important one—it lasts forever.
- Only as we live in light of eternity can we hope to live wisely today.

During my years as a Christian, I have been motivated by a number of things, some of them less than noble, but as I have grown and matured I am now motivated by one thing. One day I want to hear from the mouth of my Lord as He looks into my eyes, "Well done, good and faithful servant! You have been faithful with a few things; I will put you in charge of many things. Come and share your master's happiness!" (Matthew 25:23).

The Bible makes it quite clear that wise people seek to store up for themselves treasure in heaven rather than treasure on earth. We are actually preparing for heaven today. Each victory, each work of kindness, each godly response, each moment when we honor God by what we do, say, give, or give up is an investment into our heavenly account (Ephesians 6:8). We need to come to grips with the truth that we are already preparing for heaven—the only question is how?

While to some it may seem selfish and wrong to seek to improve our own future with our own good in mind, the Bible disagrees with those feelings. In fact, we are told time and time again to prepare for the future today (1 Timothy 6:18–19).

C. S. Lewis writes, "If there lurks in most modern minds the notion that to desire our own good and earnestly to hope of the enjoyment of it is a bad thing, I submit that this notion has crept in from Kant and the Stoics and is no part of the Christian faith. Indeed, if we consider the unblushing promises of reward and the staggering nature of the rewards promised in the Gospels, it would seem that our Lord finds our desires, not too strong, but too weak. We are half-hearted creatures, fooling about with drink and sex and ambition when infinite joy is offered us, like an ignorant child who wants to go on making mud pies in a slum because he cannot imagine what is meant by the offer of a holiday at sea. We are far too easily pleased."[2]

The Prize

We are encouraged over and over to press on toward the prize in our Christian lives. This means that the prize is not found in this life but the next. Yet how many of us truly live that way, as though we believe that our prize is ultimately in the next life? We need to heed these words again.

Do you not know that those who run in a race all run, but only one receives the prize? Run in such a way that you may win. Everyone who competes in the games exercises self-control in all things. They then do it to receive a perishable wreath, but we an imperishable. Therefore I run in such a way, as not without aim; I box in such a way, as not beating the air; but I discipline my body and make it my slave, so that, after I have preached to others, I myself will not be disqualified (1 Corinthians 9:24–27 NASB).

I press on toward the goal for the prize of the upward call of God in Christ Jesus . . . Brethren, join in following my example, and observe those who walk according to the pattern you have in us. For many walk, of whom I often told you, and now tell you even weeping, that they are enemies of the cross of Christ, whose end is destruction, whose god is their appetite, and whose glory is in their shame, who set their minds on earthly things. For our citizenship is in heaven, from which also we eagerly wait for a Savior, the Lord Jesus Christ (Philippians 3:14, 17–20 NASB).

The Nature of the Rewards

What then is the nature of the rewards we are to seek? We have already discussed the primary one, which is to receive the approval of our Lord for our life: "Well done my good and faithful servant . . . Enter into the joy of your master." But what does that mean? Author and professor Dallas Willard has a suggestion: "That joy is, of course, the creation and care of what is good in all its dimensions. A place in God's creative order has been reserved for each one of us from before the beginnings of cosmic existence. His plan is for us to develop, as apprentices to Jesus, to the point where we can take our place in the ongoing creativity of the Universe."[3]

Crowns

Rewards are often described in Scripture as crowns that we will be given. In the New Testament, two Greek words are translated "crown." One is *diadema*, a royal turban typically worn by Persian royalty. It always signified kingly or royal dignity. It refers only to the type of crown Jesus receives. The other word is *stephanos*, the victor's crown. It was a symbol of victory in the Olympic games and other contests, a reward or prize for winning. This was a beautifully woven crown of leaves or vines, and this is the word used to describe our own crowns.

In Scripture we learn of five different crowns we can win. There is the crown of life (James 1:12; Revelation 2:10), the crown of righteousness (2 Timothy 4:8), the incorruptible crown (1 Corinthians 9:25), the crown of rejoicing (1 Thessalonians 2:19), and the crown of glory (1 Peter 5:2–4).

These crowns are awarded for the lives we have lived on earth. Each one of the crowns had a special signification in Scripture:

- **crown of life**: This crown is bestowed in recognition of enduring and triumphing over trial and persecution even to the point of martyrdom. The motivation must be love for Christ.
- **crown of righteousness**: This crown is awarded to those who have completed the Christian race with integrity, with eyes fixed on the coming Lord. It is the reward for fulfilling the ministry God has entrusted to a believer.
- **incorruptible crown**: This crown is worn by those who strive for mastery, for excellence. Here Paul is using the figure of the pentathlon with its tremendous demand of physical stamina. This crown is awarded to the disciplined.
- **crown of rejoicing**: This is the crown of the soul winner. It will be cause for rejoicing when, in heaven, we meet those who have been won to Christ through our ministry. This crown is open to every believer.
- **crown of glory**: This promised award for spiritual leaders in the church should provide strong motivation for sacrificial pastoral ministry.[4]

There is much discussion among Bible scholars as to whether these are literal or figurative crowns. There is a strong case to make for each point of view. These could certainly be literal crowns that our Lord gives to us, or they could also be figurative symbols of our Lord's extreme pleasure. Pastor and author John MacArthur believes that "Believers' rewards aren't something you wear on your head like a crown . . . Your reward in heaven will be your capacity for service in heaven . . . Heaven's crowns are what we will experience, eternal life, eternal joy, eternal service, and eternal blessedness."[5] Either way, these are rewards that will have far more meaning to us than we can possibly imagine here on earth. They will be tangible benefits not given to every believer. Unlike salvation itself, these crowns are earned here on earth by our service to Him.

Greater Responsibility

What is made clear over and over in Scripture is that believers will be given greater responsibility in heaven depending on their faithfulness on earth. In several parables Jesus made it clear that faithfulness with what we have been given (our life, talents, resources, time) will determine how much responsibility we are given in heaven.

J. Oswald Sanders points out, "In the parable of the minas (Luke 19:11–27) and the talents (Matthew 25:14–30), Jesus taught that each believer has differing abilities and capacities. That is something over which we have no control and for which we are not responsible. The parable of the minas teaches that *where there is equal ability but unequal faithfulness, there will be a smaller reward. On the other hand, the parable of the talents tells us that where there is unequal ability but equal faithfulness, the rewards will be the same.*"[6]

It is encouraging to learn that rewards won't be determined by talents and abilities and resources over which we have no control but by our faithfulness with what we have been given, something over which we all have control.

Ruling and Reigning with Christ

But whenever we speak of responsibilities in heaven, the question naturally arises: For what will we be responsible? Of course we can't answer that question entirely, but we can speak of what God has revealed to us, and it is an awesome thought.

It is rarely taught but abundantly clear that believers will rule and reign with Christ forever. "He who overcomes, and he who keeps My deeds until the end, to him I will give authority over the nations" (Revelation 2:26 NASB).

"And they sang a new song, saying, 'Worthy are You to take the book and to break its seals; for You were slain, and purchased for God with Your blood men from every tribe and tongue and people and nation. You have made them to be a kingdom and priests to our God; and they will reign upon the earth' " (Revelation 5:9–10 NASB).

"If we endure, we will also reign with Him; If we deny Him, He also will deny us" (2 Timothy 2:12 NASB).

We are told that we will even judge angels. "Do you not know that we will judge angels? How much more matters of this life?" (1 Corinthians 6:3 NASB). What form this ruling and reigning will take is not completely clear. How or even why we will judge angels is a matter of speculation as well. Will we be involved in the final judgment of the fallen angels?

It is this truth of ruling and reigning with Christ and even judging angels that leads me to surmise that our growth in godliness and faithfulness in this life will have a direct correlation to our position in His new eternal kingdom.

It is very clear in Scripture that there will be a heavenly government under Christ in heaven, though if you thought only of governments today you would be depressed. But the better country will have a perfect government, for it will be run by men and women made perfect by God under Christ. There will be people over us in authority and honor as well as people under us in authority and honor. But the great news is that the governors and the governed will be perfect, initiating and responding in perfect unity.

All of us will be serving Christ first and serving each other second, not desiring power or jockeying for position. The world has never had even a taste of such a government. In our democracy, politicians delight in calling themselves "public servants," yet often act like despots. The perks of power intoxicate them, and they stop acting like servants and start enlisting them.

It is often a hard sell with Christians to talk about preparing for heaven since we are told that God will make us brand new people and we will live in a home God designed for us. It is easy to think, "I will be blissfully happy no matter what—so what difference does it make?" After all, since one day God will make me perfect—why knock myself out today trying to be transformed? Why not just wait and let Him do it in me in heaven? It all turns out the same in the end, doesn't it?

In a mystery, our lives on earth are *the only opportunity* to prepare for greater service and responsibility in heaven forever. While all will be made new and given a brand new home for all eternity beyond their wildest dreams and filled with eternal joy, not all will be able to hold certain very honored and important positions in heaven. These are attained through service and faithfulness here on earth.

Our Last Chance

This life is our only chance to attain to those precious positions and services that are reserved for those who demonstrate the greatest desire for them through sacrificial service and faithfulness here on earth.

If we love this world too much, if we are lured away from service to Christ by chasing our own desires and passions and remaining unfaithful stewards, we will enter the marvelous gates of heaven—but empty handed.

There awaits those who were truly faithful, greater rewards for service, treasure that their earthly service won for them, day by day, year by year, until their last dying breath. We are not told what this will be specifically, but we know that it will involve praise and pleasure from our Lord for our efforts. If for no other reason than to bring greater pleasure in us from our Lord, our earthly sacrifice of service would be worth it. But the clear implication of Scripture is that our rewards will, indeed, be eternal and, in some way, tangible and lasting, bringing us joy forever.

Positions that are truly desirable and responsibilities that bring the greatest pleasure and honor are reserved in eternity for those with the faith to pursue them—for that is what it takes. Most of us live for the here and now. Most of us are concerned mainly with accumulating treasure on earth, improving our portfolios here on earth, improving our positions here on earth. Indeed, much of modern Christianity, especially the burgeoning prosperity movement, emphasizes that God's great blessings are to be pursued here and now for ourselves.

But none of the apostles entertained such a vision of ministry and Christian service. Paul makes it clear that the apostles were lacking in the most basic of necessities, and not because they were bad business people or lazy or somehow lacking in the faith of modern preachers of prosperity but because they were preparing themselves for an entirely different kingdom (1 Corinthians 4:9–13; 9:1–27).

The faithful in Christ, those who are preparing for heaven who have set their eyes on things above and not on things below, are gladly willing to give up many of the pleasures and comforts this world can offer because they are convinced something better is being prepared for them (Hebrews 10:32–36). Furthermore, their hearts desire Him and seek Him more than anything else anyway.

C. S. Lewis writes, "The point is not that God will refuse you admission to His eternal world if you have not got certain qualities of character: the point is that if people have not got at least the beginnings of those qualities inside them, then no possible external conditions could make a 'heaven' for them."[7]

It is foolish to give up some of the comforts and luxuries and enjoyments we can provide for ourselves just to exercise some form of asceticism. That is merely asceticism for asceticism's sake. But Jesus urged us to lay up for ourselves treasure in heaven where moth and rust do not destroy it. In other words, Jesus was pointing out that in asking us to, at times, give up time, resources, talents, and treasures for His sake, He was calling us to be wise. Everything on earth we can chase is slated to be destroyed and remains behind when we die.

Yet the treasures He promises us will last forever. But it only makes sense through the lens of faith. If we truly grasp the reality that today we are actively storing up both treasure and honor that will be given to us by our Lord upon our arrival, any earthly sacrifice of time, talent, or treasure will be a pleasure and an opportunity. In fact, we are foolish not to make these sacrifices.

Even in our world most people come by worldly wealth by prudence and the practice of delayed gratification. They are willing to be frugal and spend less than they make, investing their resources in wise investments that reward them the most the longer they don't touch it, so that in their later years they can retire in ease and comfort, enjoying their final years.

If that is wise retirement planning when our retirement years are twenty to thirty at the most here on earth, how much wiser is it to prepare for your heavenly life when the investments pay off forever? The poorest people on earth could enjoy the greatest eternal rewards, and the richest people on earth could enter heaven with nothing to show for their earthly lives.

The Cost

"The average church member would do well," says Vance Havner, "to look in his concordance and see how many columns it takes to list all the 'serve,' 'servant,' and 'service' references."[8] We have been called to serve Christ, not just called to enter His church. Church membership will be no cause of reward in heaven. Rewards are given in heaven for service, and there is no use denying that service exacts a cost from us. You cannot truly serve God unless your service involves some sort of sacrificial element. Though the cost may sometimes be high for service and faithfulness to Christ, we must also consider the rewards for doing so.

"I consider that our present sufferings are not worth comparing with the glory that will be revealed in us" (Romans 8:18). Paul makes it clear that it isn't worth the effort of comparing any suffering or inconvenience that might occur as we serve our Lord in light of what our reward will be for doing so. If we are to seriously consider preparing for heaven now, we must count the cost. Many have done so and felt that they would rather enjoy the fleeting pleasures of this world rather than invest in the next. They are choosing poorly. It was Jim Elliot, a missionary, who said, "He is no fool who gives up what he cannot keep to gain what he cannot lose." He demonstrated his faithfulness through his martyrdom as he shared his faith with members of the Auca tribe of Ecuador, who later killed him and four other young missionaries serving with him in 1956. Some would think his life foolish, a sad waste, but God would not. He lived wisely. His reward will far outweigh his sacrifice. Unless we understand and believe that, we can never rightly prepare ourselves for heaven.

Not many of us are called to such sacrifice and service, but what sacrifice and service are we called to? Faith is the essential element in this discussion—not time, not resources, and not abilities. The issue is this: Do we really believe what the Bible says? If so, how can we live only for the here and now?

God Cannot Be Fooled

But true service to Christ has a characteristic quality about it. The Scriptures teach clearly that God knows why we do what we do. Only those things truly done for Christ will be rewarded. It is quite possible, and frequently true, that we do good things for less than noble reasons. I can seek the approval of others by my good deeds (Acts 5:1–5) while harboring sinful motivations. These will result in no reward.

"A Christian should always remember that the value of his good works is not based on their number and excellence, but on the love of God which prompts him to do these things."[9]

The apostle Paul reminds us, "He will bring to light what is hidden in darkness and will expose the motives of men's hearts. At that time each will receive his praise from God" (1 Corinthians 4:5).

Author and pastor Erwin Lutzer points out, "Some Christians refer with smug satisfaction to many years of 'faithful service' to the Lord. They are quite sure that they will receive a great reward at the judgment seat of Christ—and candidly, they think they deserve it. Obviously they have not understood the words of Christ, that the first shall be last and the last shall be first. Surprises lie ahead!"[10]

Our service won't be judged just by how much we have done or how much we have given, but by the heart and spirit in which it was given. How much of us was there in that gift? Was it our love of God that prompted these things, or a less noble motivation?

Paul creates a list in 1 Corinthians 13:1–3 of those acts that have no value if they are not done out of love for God and men. We would do well to revisit that list and ask ourselves how proud we would be if even one of these descriptions fit us. They include the following:

- speaking with the tongues of men and angels
- having the gift of prophecy
- knowing all mysteries
- having all knowledge
- having faith that would move mountains
- giving all my possessions to feed the poor
- delivering my body to be burned

Keep in mind that Paul is clearly assuming it would be possible to do or have all these marvelous things—*without* love! We are too easily bamboozled by activity that has the appearance of goodness but which often has absolutely no eternal value. You can fool people—but never God. Love is the main ingredient that must be present for anything of service to be acceptable to God and profitable for us in eternity.

Ironically, while we are called to serve Him faithfully and are promised rewards for faithful service, the truth is that we can only do that with His help. Only by His strength and gifting can we do the very things He desires; therefore, even our service to Him is a result of His grace to us. What we can offer Him is our heartfelt desire to glorify Him and honor Him in every way. It's a paradox; we can't receive any rewards unless He helps us.

While this may sound strange, it isn't that far removed from many of our own experiences. When my children were younger, at Christmas time they would ask to do chores for which they could receive money to buy presents. They were my children and should rightly have done those chores without payment as part of their family responsibility (which they all later did). But I gladly paid them generously so they could have the joy of working hard to be able to give presents not only to others but also to me.

Without my money they couldn't have gotten me the gift—yet I was happy to give it to them and happy to receive their gift. My greatest joy was their desire to show their love. The *ability* to give came from me; the *desire* to give came from them. This is how God can be both the author of all our service and gifts we give Him and the joyful recipient as well.

All rewards we will receive from our Lord for faithful service will still be based on His grace. In the parable of the minas and talents, all the servants were first given something to be good stewards of. They weren't taking these funds out of their bank accounts; they couldn't because they were slaves. They owned nothing, and they themselves belonged to their master; they had been bought with a price, as have we (1 Corinthians 6:19–20).

Ask yourself: "What do [I] have that [I] did not receive (1 Corinthians 4:7)? Life itself is both a gift and a stewardship. If someone is seeking to prepare for heaven for strictly mercenary reasons—to get as much as he can, to exert power over others, to receive honor he feels he is due—he has shown he truly doesn't understand heaven at all and definitely wouldn't really enjoy it if he got there.

In heaven as on earth, all glory belongs to God. Heaven isn't about honoring us, though God will graciously do so. It's about worshiping Him. If we are serious about preparing for heaven, we must understand this.

The Challenge

Our faith will determine what we invest in for eternity. Maybe we need to truly ask ourselves what we *really* believe? We too glibly give lip service to certain truths but don't really live as if they are true.

Do you believe there is a heaven waiting for you? Do you believe the next world is eternal and therefore far superior to this one? Do you believe what Jesus said when He warned us not to lay up for ourselves treasures on this earth, but in heaven? Do you believe we ought to really set our minds on things above and not on things on this earth? Do you believe that your works done on this earth will one day be judged to determine your eternal reward? Do you believe that you have a limited time to prepare for eternity? If you've answered yes to these questions, there is one more question to ask: Are you living as if that is true?

Has your life been changed by this truth? How are *you*, right now, preparing for heaven?

Every day we are working on a project we will one day hand in to our Lord. That project is ourselves. Besides the good works we can offer, we ourselves are being prepared. We are daily becoming more like Him or less like Him. The transformation God will finish when we reach heaven is in process today in each of our lives.

Wherever we are in that process is what we will present to Him. There are no transformational plateaus we can reach in this life where we can say, "Good enough, I'll stop here." There will always be more transformation that is necessary. This is part of our preparation for heaven.

The point I have reached in my transformation when I breathe my last breath is all I can offer Him, and part of my reward forever will be based on the progress I have made. Though we will all be made perfect, we will not have all reached the same point in transformation on earth into the image of Christ. That progress will be a significant part of my heavenly reward—as will yours.

Sadly, many Christians reach spiritual plateaus and then lose heart, lose enthusiasm, lose sight of the real purpose of our lives here on earth and go into spiritual retirement. Our lives, lived today, are to prepare others and us for eternity.

What are you really living for?

In light of eternity, how much of it will remain?

Choose wisely.

Only one pressing question remains.

The journey continues.

CHAPTER TEN

Guaranteeing Your Reservation

Anyone can devise a plan by which good people may go to heaven. Only God can devise a plan whereby sinners, who are His enemies, can go to heaven.[1] —LEWIS SPERRY CHAFER

You have come near to the better country. My hope is that the information in the preceding chapters has tantalized you, like a trailer of coming attractions. But entrance into this wonderful new world and life is by invitation only. Everyone will not see this marvelous new world; in fact, most people won't. It is a tragic thought made all the sadder by the knowledge that all are welcome and that God desires everyone to be saved.

Peter reminds us that, "He [God] is patient with you, *not wanting anyone to perish, but everyone to come to repentance*" (2 Peter 3:9, emphasis added).

Paul makes it clear that God "*desires all men to be saved and to come to the knowledge of the truth.* For there is one God, and one mediator also between God and men, the man Christ Jesus, who gave Himself as a ransom for all, the testimony given at the proper time (1 Timothy 2:4–6 NASB, emphasis added).

Jesus made it clear that we need to "enter through the narrow gate; for the gate is wide and the way is broad that leads to destruction, and there are many who enter through it. *For the gate is small and the way is narrow that leads to life, and there are few who find it*" (Matthew 7:13–14 NASB, emphasis added). What heaviness of heart He must have felt when He uttered these words, especially with the knowledge of all He would be doing to make the better country available to everyone.

But who is the doorkeeper at the narrow gate?

"Jesus said to him, 'I am the way, and the truth, and the life; no one comes to the Father but through Me" (John 14:6 NASB).

If we want to secure a reservation to the better country, we must know what is required to assure our place.

Faith Opens the Gate

Faith is the key that will unlock this gate to the better country for us, but not an uninformed faith or a faith in anything you choose. Only faith in the One who alone could have created the better country will suffice.

Faith demands an object. When we drive a car, we place faith in the makers of the car, the creators of the traffic signals that govern the roads, the roads, the makers of the cars everyone else is driving around us at high speed, and myriad other things. When we fly in an airplane, we put our faith in the designers of the aircraft, the pilots who are flying it, the mechanics who service it, the airport controllers, even the makers of the food we will eat on it.

Each one of us—Christian, atheist, agnostic, and the religious person—all walk by faith every day. Is my cell phone giving me cancer? Is the food at the restaurant I'm eating tainted or carrying bacteria? Will everyone I encounter on the road today respect the red lights and stop signs that keep them from colliding with me at high speed? Are the other drivers under the influence of a substance that impairs their judgment? Is the doctor who gave me my physical qualified and being careful enough to help keep me safe? Has my medicine been tampered with? Is the water safe to drink? We could go on and on. If you say you don't worry about such things, the reason is you are exercising faith.

The only difference between us is what we have decided to place our faith in. The religious person, the atheist, agnostic, and Christian—all walk by faith each moment of every day. Only the object of their faith differs.

Most people would dearly love to bypass this one condition necessary to inherit the better country. They would much rather see, hear, touch, taste, and experience this better country before they make any kind of binding decision regarding it. No such option is available. We have been left vivid descriptions of it by those whom God has allowed a peek and have even had God Himself come to earth from heaven and return there, but that is all.

Faith in the Wrong Thing Only Disappoints

The object of our faith needs to be so great and so perfect that it can't possibly let us down. Only the person and work of God qualify, so let's take a closer look at both.

Think of all the celebrities, sports heroes, politicians, governments, friends, teachers, parents, spouses, and institutions that you have placed your faith in. In time they either all have, or all will, let you down in small ways and big ways. Even church as an institution and Christians will let you down. They don't mean to, but they all share one common denominator; they are all imperfect. Being less than perfect means that the ability to always live up to their promises, and even their desires, is simply not within them. The apostle Paul talks about this at great length in Romans 7. Putting your faith in someone can be a scary or risky proposition.

It is hard for us to exercise faith. We have been let down so many times that we are hesitant to step out in faith one more time. We desperately want to have heaven on our own terms so that we don't have to exercise faith.

However, since God alone controls the entrance into His marvelous better country, it is a waste of time and effort to seek to impose our own conditions and expectations upon Him. It won't do us the slightest good to try to convince ourselves or Him or anyone else that heaven is open to us upon any other conditions than those He has set.

The fact is that only those who please Him will enter the better country. While knowledge of your own inadequacy and shortcomings might cause you to shrink back at this statement, you may be surprised at what God says pleases Him. "*And without faith it is impossible to please Him*, for he who comes to God must believe that He is and that He is a rewarder of those who seek Him" (Hebrews 11:6 NASB, emphasis added). It simply can't be stated much clearer than that.

So many people have the idea that doing good works or trying to be a good person will get them into heaven. If that were all it took, Jesus never would have needed to die for our sins to satisfy God's holiness. But the Bible teaches that we can't be righteous in God's eyes through that approach. Paul makes it clear that "if righteousness comes through the Law, then Christ died needlessly" (Galatians 2:21 NASB).

Even our good works are so tainted with evil that they are unacceptable to His perfect holy character. "For all of us have become like one who is unclean, and all our righteous deeds are like a filthy garment," says the prophet Isaiah (64:6 NASB). If it were merely a matter of doing good works or *trying* to obey the law of God, we could be saved by our own merits. But the Bible teaches this isn't possible.

"Because by the works of the Law no flesh will be justified in His sight; for through the Law comes the knowledge of sin" (Romans 3:20 NASB). The law of God actually condemns us, because through it we gain an understanding of God's holy character and perfect standard of righteousness. We realize that we cannot keep His holy law and fall short of His perfect standards.

"For all have sinned and fall short of the glory of God" (Romans 3:23 NASB).

"Nevertheless knowing that a man is not justified by the works of the Law but through faith in Christ Jesus, even we have believed in Christ Jesus, so that we may be justified by faith in Christ and not by the works of the Law; since *by the works of the Law no flesh will be justified*" (Galatians 2:16 NASB, emphasis added).

In fact, Paul says, "the Law has become our tutor to lead us to Christ, so that we may be justified by faith" (Galatians 3:24 NASB).

The law does two things: (1) it shows us the holy perfect nature of God; and (2) it condemns us by demonstrating how short we fall of His perfect standard. The law cannot make us perfect before God; just the opposite—it highlights our failure (Romans 4:15; Hebrews 7:19). In fact, it shows us how badly we need Jesus to be our Savior. Trying to be good enough to go to heaven is like trying to drink the Pacific Ocean or jump across the Grand Canyon. Yet even these examples fall far short of the reality.

You cannot clean a car by using filthy water and filthier rags; you can only move the dirt around. You can't secure a place in the better country by simply trying your best to be good. Placing our faith in the righteousness of Christ and the grace and mercy of our God is what God both desires and requires. Jesus is the author and perfecter of our faith (Hebrews 12:2); hence, even when our faith is weak, He accepts it and strengthens it (Mark 9:14–29).

Faith Is a Great Equalizer

When you think about it, faith is the one ingredient every human has access to and experience in. Some, by virtue of their position, can afford to give great amounts of money away in philanthropy. Others, based on their upbringing in a certain culture, have been taught the value of service to others and become involved with it. Still others, by virtue of their inherent personality, are caring and compassionate, centered on people and their needs. Then there are those who have access to religious training. But the fact remains that if the better country is gained simply by being religious or philanthropical or highly relational in personality or heavily involved in service, a great many people are at a distinct disadvantage, since none of these conditions were a part of their upbringing. They had little money, no training in a service culture, weren't by personality highly relational, and had little or no access to any religious training.

But every person has had to exercise faith and knows what it means. It is natural and instinctive to the human condition. Those who argue that faith is unreasonable and asks unreasonable things of us need to keep in mind that we use this kind of faith all the time to save people from earthly dangers.

C. S. Lewis writes, "There are times when we can do all that a fellow creature needs if only he will trust us. In getting a dog out of a trap, in extracting a thorn from a child's finger, in teaching a boy to swim or rescuing one who can't, in getting a frightened beginner over a nasty place on a mountain, the one fatal obstacle may be their distrust. We are asking them to trust us in the teeth of their senses, their imagination, and their intelligence. We ask them to believe that what is painful will relieve their pain, and what looks dangerous is their only safety. We ask them to accept apparent impossibilities: that moving the paw further back into the trap is the way to get it out—that hurting the finger very much more will stop the finger hurting—that water which is obviously permeable will resist and support the body—that holding onto the only support within reach is not the way to avoid sinking—that to go higher and onto a more exposed ledge is the way not to fall. To support all these *incredibilia* we can rely only on the other party's confidence in us—a confidence certainly not based on demonstration, admittedly shot though with emotion, and perhaps, if we are strangers, resting on nothing but such assurance as the look of our face and the tone of our voice can supply, or even, for the dog, on our smell. Sometimes, because of their unbelief, we can do no mighty works. But if we succeed, we do so because they have maintained their faith in us against apparently contrary evidence. No one blames us for demanding such faith. No one blames them for giving it. No one says afterwards what an unintelligent dog or child or boy that must have been to trust us."[2]

Faith is the thing God seeks from us, not in our own works but in His Son's work on our behalf. None of our own solutions will work, but that's why He provided the perfect solution Himself.

A. W. Tozer wrote, "For each of us the time is surely coming when we shall have nothing but God. Health and wealth and friends and hiding places will all be swept away, and we shall have only God. To the man of pseudo-faith that is a terrifying thought, but to real faith it is one of the most comforting thoughts the heart can entertain."[3]

Do Good Works Have No Value?

It's not that good works have no value to God—for surely they do. He has repeatedly told us He wants us to act in good ways, to obey His laws, to love Him, and to love our neighbors as ourselves, to be compassionate, forgiving, generous, pure in heart, and much more.

It is also far better to seek to be good rather than bad for social reasons. Those who abide by wise laws instead of breaking them and seek to serve others instead of defrauding them will make society stronger and safer.

Intrinsically, we will be happier if we stay away from bad, sinful, harmful activity. When we are kind and compassionate, our relationships are stronger, our marriages better, and our children healthier. We will enjoy far more peace of mind and health by trying to be a better person than an evil one.

There are uncountable benefits to being a good person who tries to help others. It is simply that in all these actions, we will still fall far short of perfection. The better country is not simply a "better" place; it is a perfect place for a people made perfect by Christ. And while most of us can point to good things we have done over the years, none of us would dream (in our right minds) of claiming we are perfect.

Yet that is the standard. God does not grade on a curve. He is a holy being, perfectly righteous in every way. The punishment for even one sin is death. So when we seek to do good works *in order to secure our place in heaven*, we are assuming a much lower standard than God has set. To seek to do good works to obey and honor God is right and proper, and every true Christian should do them. However, to trust in them to get you into heaven is a dangerous and mistaken idea.

Compared to other people, you and I may indeed be very good people. We may be far better than many others—maybe even most others. By our own estimation, as we compare ourselves with others, we can claim to be good. There is where we make the mistake.

God's absolute abhorrence of sin is not something we easily understand since we have become desensitized to the presence of sin in our world and in our hearts. Though we find it annoying and occasionally heart breaking, we can live with sin, and do. In fact, we cannot only live with sin, we can't live without it. Part of our infected human nature is magnetically attracted to sin.

If you think that this isn't true, you can prove the point very easily by yourself. Just make a promise to yourself that you will never lie, cheat, steal, covet something that belongs to someone else, be jealous, gossip, or sin in any way again.

Not once.

Ever.

When, not *if*, you break your promise, you will see the power sin has in and over you.

Can We Apologize Our Way Out of Punishment?

So while good works have many wonderful benefits, they do not cancel out our sins against God. We do not empty out our own prisons by promising convicted serial murderers, robbers, muggers, rapists, sexual molesters, pedophiles, embezzlers, con artists and the like that if they do a corresponding (or greater) number of good things, those good things will cancel out the bad things they have done and we will then let them go scot-free. What good thing could serial killers do that would cancel out their evil act? What good thing could sexual predators do that would nullify their victimization of innocent women and children? Their sentence in prison is a punishment, not a way of expunging their guilt.

Even when they have served their sentence, they will still be guilty of having committed the crimes. They may have "paid their debt to society," yet they will not have removed the *guilt* of their crime. Nothing a person can ever do will accomplish that.

In 1984, a man named William Beebe raped a woman named Liz Seccuro at a frat party at the University of Virginia. Beebe was never arrested for the crime. Twenty years later, as a recovering alcoholic putting into practice the ninth step of the twelve steps of the Alcoholics Anonymous program, which calls on members to make amends to those they have harmed, he sent a letter to Seccuro asking her forgiveness. He admitted he had raped her. As a result, she called the police and Beebe was arrested, tried, and sentenced to eighteen months in prison. Seccuro said that while she forgave Beebe for assaulting and raping her, "*an apology is not a substitute for punishment.*"[4]

Since we realize that nothing can undo or negate the awful crimes people can commit on earth, why would we expect that God, who is infinitely more righteous and holy and pure than any human justice system, would somehow allow good things done to cancel out evil ones? If we could just apologize our way out of punishment or seek to do good things to avoid punishment, there would ultimately be no justice.

Yet all the people who claim that they are good enough or deserve to go to heaven because of their good deeds use this same fallacious reasoning. God is not less just than we are; He is infinitely more just than we can possibly conceive. The guilt of sin is a problem for all those seeking to get into heaven on their own efforts.

Can Sin Keep Us Out of the Better Country?

There are some destinations we might want to visit but realize ahead of time have certain restrictions, such as no pets or no smoking. Heaven also has restrictions. The better country is a place of perfection; there will therefore be no sin there, ever. God does not allow sin in His immediate presence, and heaven will be the place of His immediate presence. Our sins completely disqualify every human being who was ever born except our Savior.

For the seemingly minor sin of eating a piece of fruit that was forbidden, Adam and Eve had to leave Eden forever. Their sin separated them from God, and so does ours. Now this news would be terribly disheartening, especially after all we have learned of the wonders of heaven, unless we realized that God desires all men to be saved and has provided a solution to the sin problem.

God is a holy and righteous God and is simply not able to overlook sins (Exodus 34:7). His righteous nature demands justice. Unfortunately, we have no ability to satisfy the demands of a holy God against our sins. We are sinners both by nature and by choice. Our situation was hopeless until God did the only thing that could be done. He satisfied His holy demands by giving His own life, perfect in every way, both human and divine, to pay this debt for all time for every person. The Bible tells us that Jesus' death on the cross *propitiated* God's righteous anger toward our sin. To propitiate is to satisfy, to meet the demands of. If you owed me twenty dollars and I demanded it of you, when you gave it to me I would be propitiated, satisfied. Jesus' work on our behalf is the *only* thing that propitiates God for the guilt of our sin.

"For all have sinned and fall short of the glory of God, being justified as a gift by His grace *through the redemption which is in Christ Jesus; whom God displayed publicly as a propitiation in His blood through faith.* This was to demonstrate His righteousness, because in the forbearance of God He passed over the sins previously committed; for the demonstration, I say, of His righteousness at the present time, so that He would be just and the justifier of the one who has faith in Jesus" (Romans 3:23–26 NASB, emphasis added).

"We have an Advocate with the Father, Jesus Christ the righteous; and He Himself is the propitiation for our sins; and not for ours only, but also for those of the whole world" (1 John 2:1–2 NASB).

"In this is love, not that we loved God, but that *He loved us and sent His Son to be the propitiation for our sins.*" (1 John 4:10 NASB, emphasis added).

We simply cannot get to heaven based on our own good works, for that payment is way too little and inadequate. To sin repeatedly, breaking the commandments of a perfectly holy God time and time again, and then to say, "Well, I've done more good than bad," is an offense against God, not a way to win His favor. In fact, the Bible makes it clear that from God's perspective, no one truly does good (Romans 3:10–12). To do something completely and perfectly good, you would have to be perfectly and completely good in the first place. Perfect behavior can flow only out of a perfect nature.

As an apology, though sincerely made, cannot begin to satisfy the justice required from a rapist, neither could good works, however well intentioned, make God forget His holy perfect nature and the enormity of our sin against Him. The sin must be judged, or God can no longer remain holy.

So God judged our sin, yours and mine, completely, terribly, in a monumental act that forever changed the world. He allowed Himself to bear our sins in His human perfect person on the cross. God the Father judged God the Son. It wasn't a divine slap on the wrist; it was a punishment so total, so complete, so infinite in effect and repercussion that God Himself claimed that He was propitiated, satisfied. "For Christ also died for sins *once for all, the just for the unjust,* so that He might bring us to God, having been put to death in the flesh, but made alive in the spirit" (1 Peter 3:18 NASB, emphasis added).

There has never been a sin committed in the past nor will there ever be a sin committed in the future that wasn't judged and punished on the cross of Christ. So to attempt now to try to earn your own way into the better country is nothing less than a blatant slap in the face to God. It is saying to God, in effect, that the horrible humiliating act by which He became a perfect man and lived among us and suffered and then died a horrible death at our hands, enduring the effect of eternal punishment, wasn't enough—I can do better. I can pay my own way into heaven.

No. You can't.

Not ever.

Heaven, the better country, is a gift, the result of the grace of God—not the reward for people who tried to be good.

"For *by grace you have been saved through faith*; and that not of your-selves, it is the gift of God; not as a result of works, so that no one may boast" (Ephesians 2:8–9 NASB, emphasis added).

If you insist upon earning your way into the better country by your good works, ignoring the grace and mercy of God poured out for us by Christ, you will never see it. The famous evangelist, Billy Graham, once said, "I'm not going to heaven because I've preached to great crowds of people. I'm going to heaven because Christ died on that cross. None of us are going to heaven because we're good. And we're not going to heaven because we worked. We're not going to heaven because we pray and ac-cept Christ. We're going to heaven because of what He did on that cross. All I have to do is receive Him. And it's so easy to receive Christ that millions stumble over its sheer simplicity."[5]

God has provided a better (and the only) way. Jesus' blood cleanses us from all the unrighteousness that God so hates. Not only does God forgive us our sins but also He provides for us righteousness, the righteousness of Christ as a part of our eternal inheritance (Galatians 3:27). As a result, we are no longer condemned (Romans 8:1) for our sins. When we place our faith in the grace of God and Christ's sacrifice for our sin, God is not mad at us anymore—forever!

But this is something we must receive by faith. To many people, this seems unfair. They believe that everyone should go to heaven.

Heaven Is Not the World's Birthright

Many people have been led to believe over the years that heaven is the birthright of every person, and only through doing something truly hei-nous could you lose this right—and perhaps not even then. As long as you try to keep your nose relatively clean, you have as good a shot as anyone else in getting to heaven. In one sense, they are right. You have, by your good works, as good a chance as anyone else in getting to heaven—and that is no chance at all (Titus 3:5).

The better country, heaven, is not ours *to lose*; it is only ours *to gain*. It is not something we deserve; it is a gift we can choose to receive humbly or reject proudly. The reason most people won't find themselves in the better country is because that is actually the last place they would want to be.

Most people don't want to acknowledge Jesus as Lord and God, their sovereign. They want to live in a world in which they are the center of everything and life revolves around them. They want to try to create their own heaven where life is most as they would like it to be—not as some deity wants it to be. They do not want to have to humble themselves before God or anyone else. An eternal existence in the presence of God, worshiping Him, holds no attraction for them—and never will.

When most people say they want to go to heaven, they do not have in mind the better country of the Bible but rather the fantasy country of their own imagination, where they determine their own destiny. Sadly, that's where they will end up.

There is only one better country. We may conjure up great heavens in our minds, but that is the only place they will really exist. We cannot make a real heaven—only God can. If we could make our own heaven, we already would have.

Possibly the greatest tragedy in life is how available God has made the better country and how adamantly people will refuse it. It sounds patently absurd to say that some people would rather choose hell over heaven, but it happens all the time. If people can reject the Son of God when He is in their midst doing miracles before them, they can reject a heaven where that same Son of God will reign as king and sovereign forever.

If we cannot humble ourselves before our creator and accept the complete and total forgiveness He offers us through the work of His Son on the cross, then we must pay the punishment our sins deserve ourselves. Hell must be chosen just as surely as heaven. Why would someone choose hell over heaven? It is the only place you are allowed to retain your pride and worship yourself. Pride can only be retained at an eternally tragic price.

Jesus made it clear that we cannot enter the better country unless we enter it as a child—simply, sincerely, and humbly by faith (Luke 18:15–17). The question must come to every person then: Which will I choose? My pride and desire to be the sovereign of my life, or Jesus, the savior and sovereign of the universe and king of the better country?

How Can We Be Happy If People Suffer in Hell?

There are some who have said that it would be impossible for anyone to be happy in heaven if even one person were in hell. Those suffering souls in hell would ruin the enjoyment of heaven for those who knew about their condition. There are a number of problems with this reasoning, including the notion that we will, in our transformation into the image of Christ, be unable to enjoy what He has promised us while others receive their punishment. Jesus Himself, with full knowledge of those in hell, was able to rejoice in His Father and return with joy to heaven and promise us that in heaven we would have no regrets, no tears. But there is another problem, and C. S. Lewis highlights it in his book *The Great Divorce*. Responding to this criticism, Lewis writes: "That sounds very merciful: but see what lurks behind it . . . the demand of the loveless and the self-imprisoned that they should be allowed to blackmail the universe: that till they consent to be happy (on their own terms) no one else shall taste joy: that theirs shall be the final power, that Hell should be able to veto Heaven."[6]

"There are only two kinds of people in the end," writes Lewis, "those who say to God, 'Thy will be done,' and those to whom God says in the end, 'Thy will be done.' All that are in hell choose it. Without that self-choice there could be no hell. No soul that seriously and constantly desires joy will ever miss it. Those who seek find. To those who knock it is opened." [7]

Hell, which our Lord mentions more often in the Scriptures than heaven, is not the primary subject of this book. Yet it must be clearly seen that it is the only other option available to a person. Annihilation is simply not an option. The Bible makes it clear that everyone will be resurrected, some unto eternal life, some unto eternal death in hell, in separation from God and the better country (Daniel 12:2; Revelation 20:11–12).

The question is not whether we shall live forever—but only where and how we shall live forever. Hell, like heaven, is an eternal dwelling.

You may respond, "But that's so unfair!" Is it? If God continually tries to get people to accept His mercy and grace and they turn Him down time after time, what option is left? If God forces me to believe, we no longer have free will. As we must be free to choose heaven, we must be just as free not to choose it. For each decision, the consequences are eternal.

If we ask why God doesn't do more to keep people from going to hell, we have to ask what more He could do. The infinitely perfect God of the universe, creator of heaven and earth and everything in them, created a perfect world and placed Adam and Eve in it. They were (literally) perfectly happy. When they were tempted to sin, they utilized their free will and chose willingly to disobey God, thus incurring His judgment.

Adam and Eve were sentenced to death and cast out of their perfect environment. Sin then infected every human being. God allowed sacrifices and offerings to atone for people's sins for a period of time, then He humbled Himself to become a vulnerable little baby and lived a perfect life among us, proved His deity by His miracles and words, and then allowed us to crucify Him, the only person who had lived a perfectly innocent human life and therefore was not guilty of anything.

Instead of destroying us when we prepared to crucify Him, He ransomed His perfect life to satisfy the Father's perfect holiness. He took the judgment for all our sins so we wouldn't have to be judged eternally in hell for them. Then He rose from the dead, defeating death, whereupon He offered the gift of eternal life to any who would avail themselves of His wondrous act of mercy and grace. At this point the honest person would have to ask: What more should He have done?

Though everyone *can* be forgiven, not all *want* to be. Some will simply never humble themselves to admit their need of a Savior. They won't admit they are sinners in the first place. But you can't put the blame on God when He has performed an incredibly sacrificial act to save them and tries repeatedly to throw them a life preserver and they repeatedly refuse it.

Lewis writes, "I willingly believe that the damned are, in one sense, successful, rebels to the end; that the doors of hell are locked on the inside."[8]

The theme in hell will be, "I did it my way!"

Michael Green writes, "The love of God, with arms extended on a cross, bars the way to hell. But if that love is ignored, rejected, and finally refused, there comes a time when love can only weep while man pushes past into the self-chosen alienation which Christ went to the cross to avert."[9]

But our focus is not on how to get to hell but how to get to the better country.

If every provision for us has been made, it would be silly not to take advantage of it.

Choosing Our Own Heaven Is Not an Option

As we have learned the biblical view of heaven, it would be good for us to ask ourselves what better or more perfect heaven could be imagined. What better atmosphere could be dreamed of? What better future could be planned for us? What better solution for the transformation of both people and institutions and even the physical universe could be hoped for? What is it that we would need to be happy forever in the presence of God that the biblical description leaves out?

While it is certainly true that every civilization has some idea of heaven, it does not make their alternative heavens a reality. If an idea is based on a faulty assumption, the conclusion will be equally faulty regardless of the logic used to arrive at it. Our thoughts, our ideas, our conjectures have no power to create a heaven for us—no matter how sincerely we might want them to be true.

I, for one, would sincerely love to visit the magical land of Narnia in C. S. Lewis's Narnia Chronicles and, from J. R. R. Tolkien's Lord of the Rings trilogy, Lothlorien, city of the elves, or the Shire, the country of the hobbits, for they are all appealing to me. Yet, for all my wishing, I cannot make reality out of fiction. God alone can create heaven, and since that is true, it only makes sense that we seek to understand heaven as He has revealed it.

Whatever personal changes we would want to make in heaven would diminish it, for what God creates is in every conceivable way absolutely perfect. Any change would be for the worse.

Making Your Reservation

So we come at last to the most important step. There is such a thing as a reservation book for this better country. In his letter to the Philippians, the apostle Paul mentions this book (4:3), and the book of Revelation mentions it frequently (3:5; 13:8; 17:8; 20:12, 15; 21:27), as does Psalm 69:28. It is the book of life, and all whose names are written in it are guaranteed reservations in the better country, not by virtue of their good-ness but their faith in God. Our reservation can be made only on this side of life, during our lifetime.

We are granted the opportunity to make this reservation many times as God seeks to draw us time and time again to Himself, and only by will-ful resistance do we rebuff His advances. But finally we may become like Pharaoh in the Old Testament. When God gave him opportunity after opportunity to acknowledge and obey Him, he continually hardened his heart against God. Finally God accepted this, and we read that God hard-ened Pharaoh's heart (Exodus 8:15, 32; 9:34; 10:1).

If we have rejected Christ as Savior and the mercy and forgiveness God offers us in Christ, we do not know how many more opportunities we may have. One day, after repeated attempts, God finally says enough.

As we near the end of this book, I hope it has become clear that the better country is available to you. You can't earn entrance into this marvelous world, nor do you deserve it, but Christ has paid the way and reconciled us to God through His work. This work, however, to be of any benefit must be accepted. Someone may have purchased tickets for you to a movie at the theater, but unless you accept them, pick them up, and use them, they remain worthless to you.

Making our reservation involves transferring our trust from the works we have done to the work Christ has done for us and asking and then receiving the forgiveness of God. It is an act of faith and simple trust, and at the moment we do this, we receive the gift of eternal life, our name is written in the book of life, and our citizenship is transferred from this world to the better country.

Friend, if you ever get a better offer than this—take it!

But you won't. Ever.

Take the gift and receive the new life Christ offers you; guarantee *your* reservation.

"We trust not because 'a God' exists, but because *this* God exists."[10]

The journey is almost over.

Where the Journey Ends

Each of us is presently on a journey to another country, whether we believe it or not. It is a real country, more real than anything we have experienced here on earth, for everything here on earth will one day be destroyed, but the better country will have no end. It will not decay; it will not diminish. Neither shall its inhabitants.

Our lives did not begin the moment we were conceived on this earth; they began the moment we were conceived in the eternal mind of God in eternity past. Our lives will not end the moment we die on this earth; in fact, in view of eternity, they will have scarcely begun. Today we live in the shadow of death, fearing it, fearing the end, our end. Nothing could be further from the truth. For the Christian, death has lost its sting.

Long after this world has passed into faded memory we will be more fully alive than we have ever been, living the immortal life God always intended us to live. A trillion years will pass, and it will be less than a moment in eternity, and we will still be young, for a hundred trillion years is but a grain of sand on an endless beach of eternity.

Only months before he died at the age of sixty-three of a terminal illness, C. S. Lewis wrote to an old friend in America who was also seriously ill: "Think of yourself just as a seed patiently waiting in the earth; waiting to come up a flower in the Gardener's good time, up into the real world, a real awakening. I suppose that our whole present life, looked back on from there, will seem only a drowsy half-waking. We are here in the land of dreams. But cock-crow is coming."[1]

"For those who say such things make it clear that they are seeking a country of their own. And indeed if they had been thinking of that country from which they went out, they would have had opportunity to return. But as it is, they desire a better country, that is, a heavenly one. Therefore God is not ashamed to be called their God; for He has prepared a city for them" (Hebrews 11:14–16 NASB).

Will Animals Be in Heaven?

And the wolf will dwell with the lamb, and the leopard will lie down with the young goat, and the calf and the young lion and the fatling together; and a little boy will lead them. Also the cow and the bear will graze, their young will lie down together, and the lion will eat straw like the ox. The nursing child will play by the hole of the cobra, and the weaned child will put his hand on the viper's den. They will not hurt or destroy in all My holy mountain, for the earth will be full of the knowledge of the Lord as the waters cover the sea (Isaiah 11:6–9 NASB).

The answer to this lingering question is, apparently, yes. We can make a good case and easily ascertain that animals will exist in the future eternal state (Revelation 6:2–8; 19:11, 19, 21). In fact, our Lord will appear on a white horse, as will all the armies of heaven (Revelation 19:14). In Isaiah 11:6–8, quoted above, we read of the future state of animals in the millennium. But will animal existence end there, or be perfected even more in eternity? Certainly the clear evidence is that the animal kingdom, which also is suffering from sin, will be renewed and remade as well. In Isaiah 65:25, clearly speaking of the new earth and new heavens, we have the wolf and the lamb grazing together, the lion eating straw like the ox, and the serpent eating dust. All animals have one thing in common: " 'They will do no evil or harm in all My holy mountain,' says the Lord" (Isaiah 65:25 NASB).

Other Reasons to Believe Animals Will Be in Heaven

- Animals were part of the first creation of God that He pronounced good. There is no reason to believe, therefore, that animals will not be a part of the new earth and new heaven.

- In the first destruction of the earth by water—the flood—animals were not all destroyed but quite conspicuously and purposefully saved. It appears that this could form a pattern we might expect to continue in the next destruction of the earth and the renewal to follow.

- The millennial kingdom immediately preceding the final judgment not only mentions animals, but animals involved in unearthly activity (wolves grazing with sheep, lions lying down with lambs). Animals and humans live together peacefully and harmoniously during this kingdom. This delightful concept is more beneficial for us than for the animals, I would think (who do not lead contemplative lives), leading me to believe the future status of the animals is directly related to our enjoyment of them. They are a part of our world, the part we are to rule over. Is there any reason to believe that God would suddenly *diminish* the new heavens and new earth by eliminating one of the attractions we most enjoy?

- Animals show up conspicuously in the book of Revelation at the end of time, as Christ and His army are all on white horses. Even if you see this as merely symbolic—it is significant that animals are mentioned in the scheme of end-time eschatology as being not only present but purposeful. We should ask ourselves why these animals are mentioned if indeed they have no further place after the end of this earth.

- They are part of God's creation that groans for release from the curse of sin. Remember, animals suffered from the curse of sin drastically (in fact, the sacrifice for human sins was often the life of an animal). If every other part of God's good creation will be renewed, why not the animal kingdom?

- They have always been closely associated with man in human endeavor. In fact, God even spoke through a donkey once and used a great fish to rescue Jonah from drowning. Animals have eased our burdens and saved our lives too many times to count. Will our new eternal endeavors be animal-less? If so, why?

- They were part of the world (earth) that we were to subdue and rule over. It certainly seems possible that God would allow us to finally fulfill that responsibility perfectly through eternity—as we did so imperfectly during this life.

- Animals have souls, though not *human* souls; nevertheless, God created them with a soulish life. Does this mean all animals that have died will be resurrected? No, we can't say that—but C. S. Lewis might be correct when he posits that "the personality of the tame animals is largely the gift of man—that their mere sentience is reborn to soulhood in us as our mere soulhood is reborn to spirituality in Christ—I naturally suppose that very few animals indeed, in their wild state, attain to a 'self' or ego. But if any do, and if it is agreeable to the goodness of God that they should live again, their immortality would also be related to man, not, this time, to individual masters, but to humanity . . . It may even be that each species has a corporate self—that Lionhood, not lions, has shared in the travail of creation and will enter into the restoration of all things."[1] Lewis goes on to posit that certain animals (pets) might be resurrected, not for themselves, but in and for the immortality of their masters, since their identity is derived from them. This is interesting, but speculative. Not everyone likes all their pets, so there are some inherent problems.
- Since God created such a dazzlingly amazing array of animal creations, would it seem likely that He would abandon one of His greatest creative acts? It seems far more plausible scripturally to believe that instead of abandoning it, He would—in light of the re-creation of heaven and earth—perfect and expand the animal kingdom as part of that recreation. Might we even live to see once again extinct species in eternity, or even new creatures?
- Would a part of God's creation so incredibly capable of, and often directly responsible for, bringing humans comfort, joy, and happiness—certainly one of the reasons for its creation—be missing from our eternal reward?

Does this mean our pets will be resurrected? As C. S. Lewis posits, it's possible. But this issue is problematic as well. Do pets exist in heaven? On earth we owned our pets. Will that same situation exist? What of pets that have had several owners who all loved them? We know that while we will exist as men and women in heaven, we will no longer be married (Matthew 22:30). The institution will not so much be abolished as replaced with something infinitely better. We won't cease to love or be close to our spouse forever; in reality we'll be far closer than it is possible to be today in our sin-infected worlds and lives. But we will have perfect relationships *with everyone*. Our need for close intimacy in an exclusive relationship will be gone, and we'll be able to experience emotional and spiritual intimacy with all as we experience that perfect intimacy with Christ.

In the same way, we might simply enjoy all creatures in a similar manner, no longer needing that personal attachment to just one or two creatures. This is, of course, mere speculation.

This appendix was offered not to provide a theology of animals or pets in heaven but as thoughts to contemplate with regard to an issue that is curious to many. Good men and women of the Scriptures could disagree, and do. I urge patience on this issue from both sides of the argument.

Discussion Guide

CHAPTER ONE

A Better Country

Questions for Discussion

1. When you think about heaven, what attributes of the better country come to mind? Write down as many things as you can that come to mind when you ponder the idea of heaven.

2. Is heaven
   - Something you are curious about?
   - Something you are very excited about?
   - Something you are confused about?
   - All of the above.

3. What events in your life (either good or bad) have prompted your thoughts to drift toward heaven?

4. What are some confusing or disturbing thoughts you've had about heaven that have made you wonder whether you'd like it?

5. If you were going to try to describe heaven and its wonders to someone else, what are the top five things you would mention? (Can you think of five?)

6. How would you gauge your emotional attachment to earth and this life?
   - Extremely attached
   - Strongly attached
   - Mildly attached
   - Not very attached
   - Not at all attached

7. Explain, as best you can, why you feel the way you do about earth? Have your feelings changed over time?

8. What would you miss the most on earth, and why? (Be honest here.)

9. What are the three biggest questions you have about heaven right now?

For Further Study

Read the story of the rich young ruler in Matthew 19:16–25. Try to answer the following questions.

1. In what ways can you empathize with the young ruler's response to Jesus' offer?

2. What issues in Jesus' offer do you think caused the young man's sadness?

3. How could Jesus expect the rich young ruler to respond positively to such a counter-intuitive idea?

4. Can you think of anyone else in Scripture who gave up wealth, position, and comfort to follow God? Try to name at least five, and describe what they sacrificed.

Application Question

Put yourself in the place of the rich young ruler. You now have money and respect and comfort to last your lifetime—but Jesus is giving you the same offer. How do you think *you* would respond? Do you feel that in some way you've already had to face this issue? If so, how?

Read Hebrews 11:8–10; Genesis 12:1–7; and 13:14–18. Answer the following questions.

God gave Abraham an earthly inheritance, the physical land that was to become the nation of Israel. Yet the Hebrews passage focuses on another promised land.

1. How much of the earthly promise did Abraham see fulfilled in his lifetime?

2. Which city was Abraham really looking for, and how was that city different from the earthly inheritance?

3. What does Hebrews 11:13–16 tell us about the other heroes of the faith? What were their lives really focused on?

4. Read verses 17–40. What were these heroes of the faith willing to give up in order to gain the heavenly city awaiting them?

5. What was the one common ingredient in each of their lives that enabled them to make such amazing sacrifices?

Application Question

As you look at the "Hall of Faith" in Hebrews 11, how do the heroes' examples challenge your own faith? What change does it make you want to make? What might be holding you back?

Reflection

In a quiet place and in an unhurried way, think back upon your life. Return to the moments when you were the happiest or most fulfilled or the most excited. Write down four or five of these precious moments. After you've done that, reflect upon why these moments were so priceless to you. Why do you think these events prompted such powerful emotions in you? What is the common denominator in them?

Can you imagine heaven being as wonderful as these earthly moments? Can you imagine an eternity that makes these wonderful moments pale in comparison? If so, you are beginning to understand what lies ahead in the better country.

CHAPTER TWO

Heaven on My Mind

Questions for Discussion

1. It was proposed that we have heaven on our minds when we are frustrated with life here on earth and want things to be different from how they are. How often have you found yourself longing for heaven?

2. What are some different ideas of heaven you have heard from friends, family, or acquaintances that seem born more out of human desire than biblical reality?

3. Can you think of a celebrity or personality who seemingly had everything this world could offer and yet was unhappy? Along the same lines, can you think of people you know who have so much and yet are not satisfied? Spend a few moments thinking about what the signs of discontentment really are.

4. C. S. Lewis wrote, "Most people, if they had really learned to look into their own hearts, would know that they do want, and want acutely, something that cannot be had in this world." Take a few moments and try to list at least three things that you want acutely out of this life but realize you can't have or probably won't get. What implication does that have for what you are hoping for out of this life?

5. In what ways do you think "homesickness for heaven" has been evident in your own heart?

6. Have you ever felt guilty experiencing a "holy discontentment" in your life? How would you differentiate between a "holy discontentment" in life and an "unholy discontentment" in life?

7. What would be the natural feelings for aliens and strangers in a country that was not their own? Try to list at least five feelings you think would be common among all aliens and strangers in a foreign country. Have you ever experienced these as a Christian?

8. Have you had any glimpses or tastes of heaven in your life, moments when everything, even for a short time, seemed perfect—just the way life should be—or a moment so beautiful and precious to you that you never wanted it to end? How might those moments point to what heaven will be like?

9. Read again C. S. Lewis's arguments from desire (pages 34–35) and the three ways of responding to this desire at the end of this chapter. How have you looked at this unrequited desire we all experience? Was it the fool's way, the disillusioned sensible man's way, or the Christian way? If you were to create another category to best fit your reaction, what would it be?

For Further Study

Read chapter 10 of book 3, entitled "Hope," in *Mere Christianity* by C. S. Lewis.

Read 2 Corinthians 12:1–5, Paul's account of having been taken up into heaven. Though he speaks in the third person, he is clearly referring to himself personally.

- Where did Paul say he had gone?
- Was he there in spirit or body?
- What did he hear?
- Why do you think he was not permitted to tell what he heard?
- Why do you think God gave Paul such an amazing experience?
- How do you think this experience changed Paul or helped him?
- How do you think such an experience would change or help you?

Read Philippians 1:21–24 in light of Paul's experience. What do you think was really tearing at Paul?

Look up and read again the alien and stranger passages mentioned in this chapter in your Bible (Genesis 23:4; 47:9; 1 Chronicles 29:15; Psalm 39:12; 1 Peter 2:11). How do you think people separated by experiences, culture, and even thousands of years could still have the same feelings and experiences? Is feeling like an alien or stranger on earth an *encourage*-ment to you, or a *dis*couragement? Or both? Why?

Read 2 Corinthians 5:1–9 again in your Bible. What part of this description of holy discontentment do you identify with most? How does Paul contrast our present experience with our future one? What word pictures does he use, and what do they convey to you?

Read Romans 8:23–25. What does Paul say is the thing we are eagerly awaiting? What are the implications of an earthly adoption—how do they compare with the implications of our heavenly adoption by God? How many times does Paul use the word *hope*? How does Paul view hope in this passage?

Application Task

Make up a short survey with a few questions designed to provoke thinking among your non-churched friends. See if you can get some of your friends to respond to these. (There are no right or wrong answers, so it shouldn't be intimidating for them. And don't use this as a springboard for sharing your faith unless they ask about it. This is a fact-finding survey for you.) When you look at their answers, try to discover the common ingredients in them all. How are they similar to each other? What do they tell you about the way God has made all of us?

Questions like the following:

If you had ultimate power and could change the world in three major ways, what would you change, and why?

If you had the power to make these changes, what attributes would you remove from your own life and which would you add? Again, why?

How would you make heaven on earth if you had the power?

Reflection

Imagine that you had the ultimate power to make life different on earth. Give your imagination free rein. How would you change yourself? How would you change others? What would you eliminate? What would you add? Make your list as long as you like. Take several minutes, or even hours, to slowly let these thoughts percolate as you compile your list.

Then, after you've compiled your list, look at it carefully and ask yourself what all your items have in common. What does your list say about you, your world, and your current situation? Keep this list handy as you continue through this book and check off items if you learn that they will one day be part of your life in the better country.

At the end of the book, see how many items that are on your list are not promised in the better country. Ask yourself what you are really hoping for. What about heaven most captures your interest and excitement? What does that tell you about how God made you, uniquely?

CHAPTER THREE

Heaven on Earth—*Finally*

Questions for Discussion

1. Re-read the mistaken ideas about heaven in this chapter. How many of those ideas have been sabotaging your desire for the better country? Could you add any to this list?

2. Which one of the mistaken ideas was most discouraging to you as you thought about heaven in the past? Why?

3. You may have already been aware of the biblical truth concerning the renewal of the earth and heavens, or perhaps this is the first you have heard about it. What was your initial response when you heard this truth at some point in the past or as you read this book?

4. Re-read slowly 2 Peter 3:10–13 and Romans 8:21–22 concerning how God is going to make all things new. Try to read it in several different versions of the Bible if you have them. How will it all happen? What exactly will occur? What would this amazing act of destruction and restoration be like to observe? What is the final destination of the new earth and new heaven? Who does Peter tell us made the promise that this would occur?

5. Read Psalm 102:25–26; Isaiah 65:17; Isaiah 66:22; and Hebrews 12:26–29, then turn to Revelation 21:1 and read until the end of Revelation chapter 22. How clear are these promises and their fulfillment in Revelation? Why do you think God gave these amazing promises to us? What is your personal response to them?

6. Have you been taught that all the heavenly descriptions in Scripture were either symbolic or literal? Or were you taught that they are a combination of the two? What is the reason for spiritualizing these passages? Is it still hard for you to think of these descriptions as literal, and if so, why?

7. What do you find to be the strongest argument for seeing the new earth and the new heavens as physical, tangible, literal places?

8. Do you think the new heaven and new earth will be renewed, or entirely re-created? Why do you feel the way you do?

9. We know that God walked in the garden of Eden with Adam and Eve. Based on what we know about this, what do you think this says about the relationship God will have with the promised better country to come? In other words, how can we see God's involvement with His physical creation, and what might that mean for the future?

10. What do you see as the biggest difference between lifeboat and ark theology? Which position do you think you've held in the past (if any)? Which are you leaning toward now? Why?

11. How does the thought of having a glorified body like our risen Lord's excite you? What are the most exciting implications of that truth for you? How does it affect your excitement about your eternal life in the better country?

12. This chapter quotes author Randy Alcorn on how he believes the new earth will be like the old earth on p. 41. What does he say that you do agree with, what aren't you convinced of, and what are you still wondering about?

13. How do you think the new earth and new heavens will be like the old earth and old heavens? How do you think they will be different?

14. How does the idea of the new earth and new heavens as a real place change your ideas about life in the better country? What is most exciting to you?

For Further Study

Read 1 Corinthians 15.
- What do you feel are Paul's strongest arguments for a physical and bodily resurrection of all believers?
- What is the danger for a Christian of denying the resurrection, according to Paul?
- How does Paul compare Adam and Christ?
- With what does Paul compare the resurrection of our bodies?
- What are the similarities and differences of physical and spiritual bodies, according to Paul?

Reflection

Set one day aside, or even a weekend when you have more leisure time, and take a walk or a drive. As you look at the creation around you—trees, hills, ocean, lakes, sky—begin to ask yourself what a new earth would be like that was better by far than all you are seeing. Then, think about what life would be like on that new earth with a brand new glorified body to enjoy it forever.

Let God begin to change your perspective about this present life and the life to come. As you are thinking about these things, re-read Colossians 3, especially the first four verses.

CHAPTER FOUR

Waking Up in Heaven

Questions for Discussion

1. Have you ever thought about that moment when you will die and wake up in the presence of God? If you have, what did you think it would be like? If you haven't, why not?

2. Were you aware that the Bible teaches we will be in paradise before the new heaven and new earth will be created for us? Does it make a difference to you? Why or why not?

3. In what ways do you think paradise will be very much like final heaven, the better country? In what ways do you think it will be different?

4. As you think about the idea of paradise, what thought excites you most?

5. Both Paul and John were eyewitnesses to the glory of heaven (at least as much of it as they were allowed to see and experience). How do you feel your present life would be changed if you could see what they saw? List three major ways you believe your life would be altered forever, and why.

6. Do you agree with the idea that we will have a tangible, yet non-physical, form in paradise? If yes, why? If no, why not?

7. Do you think that when we get to paradise we will be aware of what is happening on earth or not? Read Revelation 6:9–11. How much do you think we will know or see? Why do you think so?

8. Do you trust anecdotal experiences of people who claim to have seen or been to heaven (such as author Don Piper's)? Do these claims strengthen your faith, or are you skeptical? What are the positive as well as negative ramifications of such experiences? What are the limitations of all such experiences (Luke 16:31)?

9. Where do you think paradise is right now? Within our universe? In another spiritual world?

For Further Study

Read Luke 16:19–31, the story Jesus told of Lazarus and the rich man. What does this true account reveal to us about both paradise and Hades? Try to come up with at least five truths about paradise. How is it both a sobering and exciting revelation of what is to come?

Read Luke 9:28–36, the account of the transfiguration of Jesus. What does this amazing incident teach you about what life might be like for us in paradise before we receive our glorified bodies? How do you think Peter, James, and John knew that it was Elijah and Moses speaking with Jesus, since they had never seen them before?

Reflection

In light of all you have learned so far about heaven and paradise, imagine waking up in heaven. What do you think would feel and be most different—most joyful—for you? Write down all the things you would be most excited about as they occur to you. Over the next few days and weeks, add to your journal new things you will be looking forward to. Keep this list available for encouragement and personal perspective.

CHAPTER FIVE

Our Heavenly Acre

Questions for Discussion

1. What are the four most important things that define home to you?

2. What are some of your best memories of home, and why do you think they are so important to you?

3. How has your home changed over the years in both negative and positive ways? What does this tell you about the nature of all earthly homes?

4. C. S. Lewis writes about the "secret signature of each soul." Re-read this section and try to think of some ways your desires make you unique. How do you feel or hope your secret signature will affect your own home in heaven?

5. Did it ever occur to you that your heavenly home would be such an immense and wonderful place that you could go on discovering its wonders forever? How does this idea affect your thinking and desire for heaven?

6. When you read about the New Jerusalem in Revelation 21 and 22, what part of the description stands out most to you—and why?

7. What positive earthly aspects of home do you most look forward to in your heavenly home? What negative aspects of earthly home will you be most glad to be rid of?

For Further Study

Review the dimensions of the New Jerusalem in Revelation 21:15–17. Within this amazing city will be your home—prepared for you by Jesus. Let's think about it a little.

- What aspects of the dimensions of the city most surprise you?
- Do you feel these dimensions are merely symbolic, or are they to be understood literally. Why?

- If you understand these dimensions as merely symbolic, what do you feel they symbolize, and what is the purpose of such grand symbolism?
- What is most attractive and exciting to you about the layout of this amazing city?
- What part of living within this city are you most excited about?
- What similarities to your earthly home can you find in the description of the New Jerusalem?

Reflection

Walk around your home (or, if you are away from your home, take a mental walk through it) and write down what makes it so special to you. If you've lived in several homes, pick out your favorite parts of each one of them and put them on your list. Include the family members, friends, and neighbors who make up home to you. Don't forget to write down those physical characteristics of home as well.

Include all those things that move you emotionally, even if you aren't sure why they do (a piece of furniture, a special painting, a special window seat in the bedroom, certain smells or sights).

Now, allow yourself to ponder the fact that these things move you because God made you that way. God, who made you so uniquely, will create a home for you that, as C. S. Lewis says, will be made for you "stitch by stitch as a glove is made for a hand."

CHAPTER SIX

The Real Magical Kingdom— The Atmosphere of Heaven

Questions for Discussion

1. Have you ever seriously thought about the atmosphere of heaven? What did you think it might be like?

2. From what you have learned about the atmosphere of heaven, what do you think your first emotion will be when you experience it—and why?

3. Read Psalms 16:11 and 21:6. How do these verses help to explain the atmosphere of heaven? What is joy connected to?

4. John MacArthur writes, "As sinners we are naturally prone to think a little sin is surely more enjoyable than perfect righteousness. It is hard for us to imagine a realm wholly devoid of sin and yet filled with endless pleasures." Why do you think this is true?

5. How many people are you expecting to see in heaven? On what ideas or Scriptures do you base your belief?

6. As you think about the renewed and perfected citizenry of heaven, what three characteristics in others are you most looking forward to? How do you think this will make our new heavenly society so different from our present earthly society?

7. What changes in yourself do you most look forward to in eternity, and why?

8. How do you think having an unlimited amount of time will affect life for you in eternity? What will it enable you to do that you can't today? Can you think of some ways that having unlimited time would make a huge impact on life today on earth? On your life specifically?

9. How do the limitations of time bring stresses into your life here on earth in specific ways?

10. When you think about the sounds of heaven, what do you most want to hear?

11. Do you think there will be crying in heaven? Make your case, pro or con.

12. Does the idea of serving in heaven excite you? What do you think some of our service might consist of toward Him, toward each other?

13. What would you add to the list of topics you'd like to talk with our Lord, others, or even angels in heaven about?

For Further Study

Read Matthew 17:1–8, Luke 16:19–31, 2 Corinthians 5:6–8, Philippians 1:23, and Revelation 6:9–11. Do you think these passages make it clear we will be conscious immediately after death? Can you think of any other passages that either support or challenge this idea?

Re-read the description of the New Jerusalem (pages 86–89 and Revelation 21–22). What aspect of the New Jerusalem are you most:
>Surprised by?
>Excited about?
>Confused by?
>Impressed with?

Read Genesis 11:1–9 about the Tower of Babel. How do you see the eternal state being a final solution to the Tower of Babel judgment? How did everyone speaking the same language create strengths and weaknesses in mankind? How would everyone speaking the same language be a strength in eternity?

Read the appendix at the end of the book on animals in heaven.
- Defend your belief about whether you think there will be animals in heaven.
- Do you think our pets will be in heaven? Why?
- Do you think there will be new animals in heaven? Why or why not?
- How might our relationship with animals be different in heaven from how it is now on earth?

- How do you see the animals themselves being different in heaven from how they are here?

Reflection

When we are planning a vacation to a place we're eager to visit, we often write down a number of things we most want to do and see when we get there and share them with our friends. Based on what we've just studied about the atmosphere of heaven, write a letter to the Lord listing the things you most want to experience when you arrive in heaven and why those things will be so special to you. Keep this letter and add to it when you learn other things about heaven you didn't know.

CHAPTER SEVEN

In His Presence

Questions for Discussion

1. God becoming a man is an amazing concept. What is the most incredible part of that truth to you?

2. What do you think we learned about God through the life of Jesus that we couldn't see as clearly in the Old Testament? What do you think was the *most important* thing we learned about God when He became a man?

3. The incarnation, God becoming a man in Christ Jesus, is what will allow us one day to embrace Jesus in bodily form in heaven. How does this truth affect your desire to enter the better country with God?

4. Even though we realize that God is everywhere present at once, we still *feel* distant from Him at times. Describe your thoughts at the prospect of having a private audience with Him any time you want in heaven and of always being in His immediate presence?

5. Which best describes your feelings at having a private audience with God—and why?
   • terribly frightened
   • worried
   • unsure
   • mildly excited
   • excited
   • happy beyond words
   • _____ (your own description)

6. Try to think of how different your life would be today if you lived every second of every minute in complete awareness of and in the actual physical proximity of God in human form? How do you think living in His direct presence here on earth with our sinful natures would be different from living in His direct presence in heaven when we have been perfected?

7. If God were to do for us what He did for Elisha in 2 Kings 6:15–17, what do you think we'd be seeing?

8. Today it is difficult for us to focus completely on our Lord's presence because we are distracted so much by our world and our own sinful natures. How will it be different in heaven, and why?

9. In our world, no matter how much we may love someone, we can become bored with that person if we are with him or her all the time. Why won't we ever get bored with Jesus in heaven?

10. Is it sometimes hard for you to speak with God in prayer? What are some of the things that make it hard? How will speaking with God in heaven be totally different from speaking with Him today?

11. What surprises you the most about the fact that God wants you in His immediate presence forever?

12. The Bible teaches that all believers will be married in heaven—to Jesus. How will our marriage in heaven to Jesus be similar to our earthly marriages? How will it be different? How will it be *better by far*?

13. How do you think it will be easier to receive and recognize God's love in heaven than it is now?

For Further Study

Read Romans 3:22; 5:1, 8–11; 8:1; 10:3–4; 2 Corinthians 5:21; Ephesians 2:8–9, 13–22; 3:11–12; Titus 3:4–5; and 1 Peter 3:18.

- Based on these passages, what should be our attitude in approaching a private audience with Jesus in heaven?
- What is the basis of our peace with God?
- Are we saved by grace or by our good works?
- Is peace with God a subjective feeling that we may or may not have—or something different?
- Do you have confidence to come before God in prayer? On what basis?

Read the story of the prodigal son (Luke 15:11–32).

- Describe in your own words the reaction of the father to the son's return.
- What was the basis of the father's acceptance and restoration of his son?

- What did the father require the son to do to receive his forgiveness and love?
- What can we learn about God's attitude toward us from this parable?
- Have you ever pictured God being that excited to see you? Why? Why not?
- What is the hardest part of the father's response for you to understand?

Read Matthew 17:1–2 (the transfiguration of Christ); Revelation 1:13–17; 2:18; 4:2–3; 5:5–6; and 19:11–16. Each of these passages gives a unique description of Jesus.

- Why do you think our Lord chooses to reveal Himself in different ways to us in both the Old and New Testaments?
- What does that teach us about how God will reveal Himself to us forever in heaven, and why?
- Do these descriptions disturb or encourage you? Why?

Read Revelation 2:17.

- What do you think is the significance of the white stone every believer will be given with their new name on it? What do you think the new name will represent for you?

Read Revelation 22:4.

- Do you think that God will literally put His name on our foreheads? Why or why not?

FOCUS

Try to remember four or five of the most meaningful times of conversation and friendship you have ever experienced in your life. What made these times or situations so memorable to you? What were the common denominators present in all those moments or times? Spend some time thinking about what it will be like to live in God's perfect presence forever. How will living in His perfect presence forever be like some of your most memorable moments with others on earth—but better by far?

Now write out a personal prayer to God, telling Him how much you are looking forward to living in His direct and intimate presence forever in heaven and why. Leave room at the end to add more reasons why you are looking forward to this as they occur to you in the days, months, and years ahead.

CHAPTER EIGHT

Transformation . . . Complete!

Questions for Discussion

1. "None of us is really who we were meant to be." As you think more about this statement, what are the implications of it for your own life?

2. Have you ever felt that you never had the chance to reach your full potential? If so, what were the things that held you back?

3. Does the idea that the real you, the you God always meant you to be, has yet to be revealed
   - encourage you?
   - confuse you?
   - frustrate you?
   - excite you?
   - other?
   Explain your answer.

4. What are some of the clearest ways you can recognize yourself resisting becoming the person God wants you to be?

5. In what ways have you always wished you were different or better or stronger?

6. What gifts, abilities, or passions has God revealed to you in embryo in this life that you will be excited to see Him perfect in you in the better country?

7. How had you thought your life would turn out differently from how it has? What are your greatest regrets?

8. Has learning about your ultimate transformation by Christ given you new hope? How does that change your outlook today?

9. Make a list of some of the things in your life that you desire that you shouldn't. Then make a list of those things you don't desire as much as you know you should. Make a third list of those areas in which you've experienced the most transformation into the image of Christ.

Where have you seen the most progress? Where do you see the greatest need?

10. What do you think will be the three greatest effects of gaining a perfected mind?

11. As you think of receiving a perfected mind, what are you most excited about?

12. Try to think of five things about your new glorified and perfected body that you look forward to most—and why.

13. When you think about being able to respond perfectly emotionally, what comes most quickly to your mind?

For Further Study

Read Ezekiel 11:19–20 and 36:26–27. What does God promise to add to our lives? What does He promise to remove? What do these verses promise the results will be? When do you think this takes place?

Read Ephesians 4:17–24. How does Paul describe the mind that is not being renewed? How then does he describe the way to renewing our mind?

Read Colossians 2:1–4. Where does Paul say all the treasures of wisdom and knowledge may be found? Where does our world tell us all knowledge can be found?

Focus

Transformation is not something that God will accomplish someday in our lives but something He has already begun and will one day perfect and finish.

Think about those areas where God has already begun transformation in you. Make a short list of the ways you've seen God begin to change you. Now, with this list in front of you, ask God to reveal to you ways that you may be resisting this transformation. Ask Him to give you the strength, power, and desire to cooperate in this transformation. Then write down one specific thing you can do to cooperate with Him that you aren't doing. Make this one thing the object of your prayer before Him. Only God can change our hearts—see what He can do if we ask!

CHAPTER NINE

Preparing for Heaven

Questions for Discussion

1. Up to this point in your life, how would you say you have been preparing for heaven?

2. What are some less than noble motivations you've had for some of the good things you have done?

3. Before you read this chapter, what did you envision the rewards of heaven to be?

4. Which of the crowns described in this chapter do you feel you would most like to earn, and why?

5. Does the thought of receiving greater responsibility and honor in heaven as a result of your faithful earthly service excite or concern you? Why?

6. How do you think our heavenly government under Christ will be markedly different from our earthly ones?

7. If you knew you had only one year to live, do you think you would prepare for heaven any differently from how you have in the past? What changes would you make?

8. What is the hardest part for you about preparing for heaven *today*?

9. What are some of the very real costs of preparing for heaven in our lives today? Try to think of at least three.

For Further Study

Read 1 Corinthians 3:10–15.

- What is the foundation upon which all our good deeds must be based?
- What are the types of things Paul says we can try to build within our lives?
- What do you think each ingredient might refer to?
- How will the quality of each one of our works be evidenced?

- What do verses 14 and 15 reveal about what this judgment is concerned with as opposed to Revelation 20:11–15 (the great white throne judgment)?

Read Matthew 25:23.

- Try to think of five things that God has given to you to be faithful with until you see Him again.
- What could you do in each of these areas to become more faithful?

Read 1 Timothy 6:17–19.

- How does Paul say we can use the financial resources He has given us to prepare for eternity?

Read all the passages relating to our crowns on page 139 and following.

- Make a case for your belief that these crowns are either (1) literal or (2) symbolic or figurative.
- Ask yourself what difference it will make in your life today whether these crowns are literal or merely figurative.

Read Acts 5:1–5.

- Why were Ananias and Sapphira's good deeds not acceptable to God?
- What can we learn about the kind of works we can offer up to God?

Focus

Re-read the challenge on page 147. After taking some time to reflect on these statements that we often say that we really believe, write down the things that *you* really believe about God, heaven, and the next life.

Write a series of "I believe that . . ." statements. After you've written them down, look them over carefully and ask yourself the question: If I really believe these things, then what I really need to do is _____

_____.

CHAPTER TEN

Guaranteeing Your Reservation

Questions for Discussion

1. Of all the things God could require of us to receive guaranteed reservations in heaven, why do you think God requires faith in Him?

2. What do you think are the three most important things in life most people place their faith in? Why do you think they place their faith in these things?

3. What are the three things in life you place the greatest faith in? Why do you place your faith in these things?

4. What are some things (people, institutions) that you have placed your faith in over the years that have disappointed you? How did they let you down? How hard does it make it now for you to place your faith in God?

5. Why is trying to be good a noble and virtuous thing to do but inadequate in order to secure a place in God's better country?

6. How is faith the great equalizer?

7. How powerful do you feel sin's control is in your life?

8. What is the only thing that the Bible says will satisfy (propitiate) God's righteous judgment against our sins (1 John 2:1–2)? Why did God have to make the sacrifice Himself?

9. Why do you think most people believe that heaven is people's birthright that can only be lost if they are truly heinous in their behavior? How would you answer that assertion yourself?

10. After reading this chapter, do you think most people really want to go to this better country where Jesus is Lord and the only object of worship? Why or why not?

11. Do you believe your name is written in the Lamb's book of life? Why or why not? What evidence would you give?

12. What have you been placing *your* faith in to secure your reservation to the better country?

For Further Study

Read 2 Peter 3:9–13.

- Why has God taken so long to return to earth?
- What does God *not* want?
- What does God *want*?
- What will the Lord's coming be like?
- What does the image He portrays convey to you?
- How is the destruction of heaven and earth described?
- What do verses 11–13 tell us ought to be our response to this amazing promise of God?

Read 1 Timothy 2:3–6.

- Again, what does God truly want?
- Who is the only mediator between man and God?
- What did our mediator do for us that we couldn't do for ourselves?
- Why couldn't someone else be our mediator instead of Jesus (Hebrews 9:11–28; 1 Peter 3:18)?

Read Matthew 7:13–14 and Luke 13:22–30.

- In the Luke passage, what question was asked of Jesus?
- What was His answer?
- For those who find themselves left out of the better country, what are their responses when they finally realize their tragic mistake?
- What is the narrow door through which you can enter the kingdom (John 14:6; Acts 4:12)?

Read Hebrews 11:1–6.

- How does the writer describe the nature of true faith?
- What are things we take by faith (v. 3)?
- Before someone can truly come to a saving faith in God, what two things must they believe (v. 6)?

Read Galatians 2:16–21.

- How can a person be justified (declared righteous and acceptable) before God?
- What does verse 16 say will not justify us before God?
- Paul makes it clear that Jesus would have died needlessly if something were true? What is that?

Read Romans 3:19–28.

- Who does Paul say is accountable to God (v. 19)?
- What does Paul say brings about our understanding of our sin before God (v. 20)?
- Apart from *what* has the righteousness of God been manifested (v. 21)?
- What does every single person who ever lived (besides Jesus) have in common (v. 23)?
- Paul makes it clear that a person is justified as a gift by His what (v. 24)?
- In whom must we place our faith for God to give us His grace (v. 26)?

Read Galatians 3:22–26.

- What have the Scriptures done to everyone (v. 22)?
- What does Paul say the purpose of the law of God really was (vv. 24–25)?
- How does this understanding of the purpose of God's law differ from what you may have believed at one time?
- How does anyone become a child of God (v. 26)?

Reflection

This may be the most important reflection of your entire life. It is not enough to know that heaven exists or that the better country will be greater than our greatest hopes. It is not even enough to know that Jesus died in order to secure your spot in the better country. Unless you act upon what you know, it will all be for nothing (Matthew 7:24–27). In James 2:19, we read that even the demons in hell believe there is a God, but they do not have saving faith.

Find a quiet place and time where you can have undisturbed prayer with God. Then, think hard about what you've learned throughout the book, and especially this last chapter. If you aren't sure that you have a reservation to the better country and you want to go there, you must ask the Gate Keeper, Jesus, to grant you entrance and write your name in His book of life.

A simple prayer, sincere and heartfelt, with as much faith as you can muster at the moment is sufficient. A prayer as simple as this: "Lord, I've finally understood how much you love me and all You have done to cancel out and forgive my sins through Your death on the cross. I ask that You would forgive me, a sinner, and grant me entrance into the better country by Your grace and mercy. I realize I don't deserve it; I am trusting entirely in Your grace."

If you mean what you pray, then God is faithful and will write your name in His book. The better country has now become *your* new country! If, on the other hand, you already had a relationship with God through Christ and His work on your behalf, take this time to thank Him for making such a place and sacrificing everything to enable you to go there. Think about the fact that your name exists in His book, and one day it will be read off as you enter the better country.

Endnotes

PART ONE

Heavenly Desire: *The thing we've always wanted*

Chapter One: A Better Country

1. Joseph Stowell, *Eternity: Reclaiming a Passion for What Endures* (Grand Rapids, Mich.: Discovery House Publishers, 2006), 41.

2. *Draper's Book of Quotations for the Christian World* (Wheaton, Ill.: Tyndale House Publishers, Inc., 1992), #5629.

3. Peter Kreeft, *Heaven: The Heart's Deepest Longing* (San Francisco: Ignatius Press, 1980), 164.

4. Mark Twain, *Letters from the Earth* (New York: Fawcett, 1964), 17.

5. Mark Twain, *Adventures of Huckleberry Finn* (Mahwah, N.J.: Watermill Classic, 1988), 3.

6. C. S. Lewis, *The Last Battle* (New York: Harper Trophy, 1984), 196.

Chapter Two: Heaven on My Mind

1. C. S. Lewis, *Mere Christianity* (New York: The MacMillan Company, 1952), 106.

2. "Quotable Quotes," *Reader's Digest*, March 2006, 81.

3. Tom Brady, interview by Steve Kroft, *60 Minutes*, CBS, November 6, 2005. http://www.cbsnews.com/stories/2005/11/03/60minutes/main1008148.shtml (accessed March 4, 2008).

4. Ricky Martin, interview, *People*, Associated Press, http://music.yahoo.com/read/news/24662271 (accessed March 4, 2008).

5. Winona Ryder, interview by Associated Press, CNN.com, October 13, 2000. http://archives.cnn.com/2000/SHOWBIZ/Movies/10/13/arts.us.winona.ryder.ap/index.html (accessed March 4, 2008).

6. Karen Crouse, "Olympian Rises from Despair," *OC Register*, August 11, 1993.

7. C. S. Lewis, *The Pilgrim's Regress* (Grand Rapids, Mich.: Eerdmans, 1958), 128.

8. Peter Kreeft, *Heaven: The Heart's Deepest Longing* (San Francisco: Ignatius Press, 1980), 105.

9. Lewis, *Mere Christianity*, 119.

10. *Draper's Book of Quotations for the Christian World* (Wheaton, Ill.: Tyndale House Publishers, Inc., 1992), #7516.

11. Thomas Howard, *Christ the Tiger* (Philadelphia: J. B. Lippincott Co., 1967), 128.

12. Kreeft, *Heaven*, 66.

13. C. S. Lewis, *The Problem of Pain* (New York: MacMillan Publishing Company, Inc., 1962), 115.

14. Kreeft, *Heaven*, 65.

15. Erwin Lutzer, *One Minute After You Die* (Chicago: Moody Press, 1997), 56.

16. Lewis, *Mere Christianity*, 105–106.

PART TWO

Heavenly Location: *The world we've always longed for*

Chapter Three: Heaven on Earth—*Finally*

1. John Eldredge, *The Journey of Desire: Searching for the Life We've Only Dreamed Of* (Nashville, Tenn.: Nelson, 2000), 111.

2. Randy Alcorn, *Heaven* (Wheaton, Ill.: Tyndale House Publishers, Inc., 2004), 126.

3. Alcorn, *Heaven*, 120.

4. Henry C. Thiessen, *Lectures in Systematic Theology* (Grand Rapids, Mich.: Wm. B. Eerdmans Publishing Company, 1976), 516.

5. C. S. Lewis, *Mere Christianity* (New York: The MacMillan Company, 1952), 106.

6. Louis Berkhof, *Systematic Theology* (Grand Rapids, Mich.: Wm. B. Eerdmans Publishing Co., 1981), 737.

7. Alcorn, *Heaven*, 78–79.

Chapter Four: Waking Up in Heaven

1. Louis Berkhof, "The Final State," in *Systematic Theology* (Grand Rapids, Mich.: Wm. B. Eerdmans Publishing Co., 1981), 737.

2. Erwin Lutzer, *One Moment After You Die* (Chicago: Moody Press, 1997), 78.

3. C. S. Lewis, *The Last Battle* (New York: MacMillan Publishing, 1956), 183–84.

4. Joseph Stowell, *Eternity: Reclaiming a Passion for What Endures* (Grand Rapids, Mich.: Discovery House Publishers, 2006), 7. Dr. Stowell is quoting a chaplain on a golf tour speaking to professional golfer, Paul Azinger, who just learned he had a life-threatening cancer.

Chapter Five: Our Heavenly Acre

1. Jane Austen in *Draper's Book of Quotations for the Christian World* (Wheaton, Ill.: Tyndale House Publishers, Inc., 1992), #5843.

2. C. S. Lewis in *Draper's Book of Quotations*, #2293.

3. Joseph Stowell, *Eternity: Reclaiming a Passion for What Endures* (Grand Rapids, Mich.: Discovery House Publishers, 2006), 74.

4. C. S. Lewis, *The Problem of Pain* (New York: MacMillan Publishing Company, 1962), 147–148.

5. *Barnes Notes*, vol. 14, *Revelation*. (Reprint. Grand Rapids, Mich.: Baker Books, 1996), 454–455.

6. Randy Alcorn, *Heaven* (Wheaton, Ill.: Tyndale House Publishers, Inc., 2004), 158.

7. William Hendriksen, *More Than Conquerors: An Interpretation of the Book of Revelation* (Grand Rapids, Mich.: Baker, 1961), 249.

8. Erwin Lutzer, *One Minute After You Die* (Chicago: Moody Press, 1997), 84.

9. C. S. Lewis, *The Last Battle* (New York: Collier Books, 1956), 137.

10. Peter Kreeft, *Heaven: The Heart's Deepest Longing* (San Francisco: Ignatius Press, 1980), 67.

11. John MacArthur, *The Glory of Heaven* (Wheaton, Ill.: Crossway Books, 1996), 140–141.

12. A. A. Hodge, *Evangelical Theology* (Carlisle, Penn.: Banner of Truth, 1976), 400.

13. Alcorn, *Heaven*, 160–161.

14. J. B. Phillips in *Draper's Book of Quotations*, #6110.

15. Anonymous in *Draper's Book of Quotations*, #2399.

Chapter Six: The Real Magical Kingdom—The Atmosphere of Heaven

1. C. S. Lewis in *Draper's Book of Quotations for the Christian World* (Wheaton, Ill.: Tyndale House Publishers, Inc., 1992), #2315.

2. John MacArthur, *The Glory of Heaven* (Wheaton, Ill.: Crossway Books, 1996), 68.

3. John F. Walvoord, *The Revelation of Jesus Christ* (Chicago: Moody Press, 1966), 325.

4. Walvoord, *The Revelation*, 322.

5. Dr. Alan Johnson, *Expositor's Bible Commentary*, Frank E. Gaebelein, general editor. (Grand Rapids, Mich.: Zondervan Publishing House, 1981), 599.

6. Angelus Silesius in *Draper's Book of Quotations*, #5667.

7. J. R. R. Tolkien, *The Fellowship of the Ring* (New York: Ballantine Books, 1965), 305.

8. J. B. Phillips, *New Testament Christianity* (New York: The MacMillan Company, 1957), 7.

9. David Head in *Draper's Book of Quotations*, #5661.

10. Peter Kreeft, *Heaven: The Heart's Deepest Longing* (San Francisco: Ignatius Press, 1980), 93.

11. Albert Barnes, *Barnes Notes*, vol. 14, *Revelation*. (Reprint. Grand Rapids, Mich.: Baker Books, 1996), 455.

12. Ray Stedman, "The City of Glory." Message no. 23 from series on Revelation. The Ray C. Stedman Library. http://www.raystedman.org/revelation/4211.html (accessed March 10, 2008).

13. Martin Luther in *Draper's Book of Quotations*, #5652.

PART THREE

Heavenly Life: *The life we were always meant to live*

Chapter Seven: In His Presence

1. *Barnes Notes, Notes on the New Testament* (Grand Rapids, Mich.: Baker Books, 1996), 455.

2. C. S. Lewis, *George MacDonald: An Anthology* (New York: Macmillan, 1978), 8–9.

3. Joni Eareckson Tada, *Heaven: Your Real Home* (Grand Rapids, Mich.: Zondervan, 1996), 94–95.

Chapter Eight: Transformation . . . *Complete!*

1. C. S. Lewis, *God in the Dock* (Grand Rapids, Mich.: Wm. B. Eerdmans, 1994), 52.

2. The rich theological term *justification* means to be declared legally righteous by God because of the work of Christ on our behalf and to be treated as such. It deals not with our present holiness but with a legal standing before God. It can be found many places in the book of Romans and throughout the epistles (Romans 3:23–24, 28; 5:1; 8:30).

3. J. Oswald Sanders, *Heaven: Better by Far* (Grand Rapids, Mich.: Discovery House Publishers, 1993), 79.

PART FOUR

Heavenly Preparation: *The goal we were always meant to pursue*

Chapter Nine: Preparing for Heaven

1. C. S. Lewis, *The Problem of Pain* (New York: MacMillan Publishing Company, Inc., 1962), 145.

2. C. S. Lewis, *The Weight of Glory* (San Francisco: Harper San Francisco, 2001), 26.

3. Dallas Willard, *The Divine Conspiracy: Rediscovering Our Hidden Life in God* (San Francisco: Harper San Francisco, 1998), 378.

4. J. Oswald Sanders, *Heaven: Better by Far* (Grand Rapids, Mich.: Discovery House Publishers, 1993), 85–87.

5. John MacArthur, Jr., *Heaven* (Chicago: Moody Press, 1988), 114–115.

6. Sanders, *Heaven*, 82–83, emphasis added.

7. C. S. Lewis, *Mere Christianity* (New York: MacMillan, 1952), 77–78.

8. *Draper's Book of Quotations for the Christian World* (Wheaton, Ill.: Tyndale House Publishers, 1992), #10185.

9. St. John of the Cross in *Draper's Book of Quotations*, #10115.

10. *Draper's Book of Quotations*, #10182.

Chapter Ten: Guaranteeing Your Reservation

1. *Draper's Book of Quotations for the Christian World* (Wheaton, Ill.: Tyndale House Publishing, 1992), #5632.

2. C. S. Lewis, *The World's Last Night and Other Essays*, "On Obstinacy in Belief" (San Diego, Calif.: Harvest Books, 2002), 23–24.

3. *Draper's Book of Quotations*, #201.

4. Associated Press, "Man Gets 18 Months for '84 Attack," by Kristen Gelineau, March 16, 2007. http://www.msnbc.msn.com/id/17653968/ (accessed March 12, 2008).

5. *Draper's Book of Quotations*, #5653.

6. C. S. Lewis, *The Great Divorce* (San Francisco: Harper San Francisco, 2001), 135.

7. Lewis, *The Great Divorce*, 75.

8. C. S. Lewis, *The Problem of Pain* (New York: MacMillan Publishing Co., Inc., 1962), 127.

9. *Draper's Book of Quotations*, #4781.

10. Lewis, *The World's Last Night*, 29–30.

Epilogue: Where the Journey Ends

1. C. S. Lewis, *Letters to an American Lady* (Grand Rapids, Mich.: Eerdmans, 1967), 116.

Appendix: Will Animals Be in Heaven?

1. C. S. Lewis, *The Problem of Pain* (New York: MacMillan Publishing Co., Inc., 1962), 141–142.

Note to the Reader

The publisher invites you to share your response to the message of this book by writing Discovery House Publishers, Box 3566, Grand Rapids, MI 49501, USA. For information about other Discovery House books, music, or videos, contact us at the same address or call 1-800-653-8333. Find us on the Internet at http://www.dhp.org/ or send e-mail to books@dhp.org.